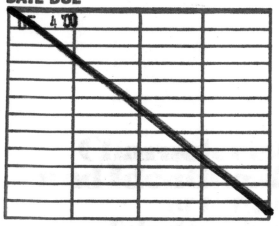

The Authors

Frederick B. Tuttle, Jr., is the Director of Curriculum and Instruction for the Wareham Public Schools, Massachusetts, and an educational consultant in gifted education and written composition. Among his publication are *Composition: A Media Approach, Technical and Scientific Writing* (with Sarah H. Collins), *Gifted and Talented Students,* and *Program Design and Development for Gifted and Talented Students* (with Laurence A. Becker), published by NEA.

Laurence A. Becker, a former high school English teacher, is an Educational Consultant in Creative Learning Environments, leading workshops throughout the United States in creativity, filmmaking, and teacher training for work with gifted learners.

The Consultants

Dr. Paul D. Plowman, Consultant and Federal Integrative Education Project Director, California State Department of Education, Sacramento

Dr. Joseph S. Renzulli, Professor of Educational Psychology, School of Education, University of Connecticut, Storrs

Dr. Dorothy Sisk, Professor, Gifted Child Education, University of South Florida, Tampa

William G. Vassar, Consultant for Gifted and Talented, Connecticut State Department of Education, Hartford

The Advisory Panel

Dr. John A. Grossi, Director, Gifted and Talented, The Council for Exceptional Children, Reston, Virginia

Deanna M. Gutschow, ESEA Title IV-C Project Director, Gifted Writing Program, Whitefish Bay Schools, Wisconsin

J. Beatrice Hall, Consultant, Education of Gifted and Talented, Austin, Texas

William C. Morgan, teacher of Gifted and Talented, Plymouth High School, Plymouth, North Carolina

Judith M. Plummer, teacher, Gifted Education Program, Mitchell School, Woodbury, Connecticut

Characteristics and Identification of Gifted and Talented Students

Second Edition

by Frederick B. Tuttle, Jr.
Laurence A. Becker

National Education Association
Washington, D.C.

Stock No. 0732-8-10

Library of Congress Cataloging in Publication Data
Tuttle, Frederick B.
Characteristics and identification of gifted and
talented students.

Bibliography: p.
1. Gifted children. 2. Talented children.
3. Students, Rating of. I. Becker, Laurence A.
II. Title.
LC3993.T83   1983   371.95   83-13132
ISBN 0-8106-0732-8

Acknowledgments
The following materials are reprinted with permission from the sources indicated: Excerpt from "Identifying American Indian Gifted and Talented" by Tom Peacock, paper presented at American Indian Gifted and Talented Planning Consortium, Bemidji, Minnesota, November 1978. Definitions from "A Model: Planning, Designing, and Evaluating Identification and Instructional Programs for Gifted, Talented, and/or Potentially Gifted Children" by Ann Lamkins, State Education Department, University of the State of New York, Albany; copyright © 1977 by Ann Lamkins and New York State Education Department. "Characteristics of Creative-Gifted Children" by Ann Fabe Isaacs, National Association for Creative Children and Adults, 1976. "Some General Characteristics of Gifted Children" from *Principles, Objectives, and Curricula for Programs in the Education of Mentally Gifted Minors — Kindergarten through Grade Twelve* by Paul Plowman and others, California State Department of Education, Sacramento, 1971. Behaviors in Six Talent Areas from "Talent Category Explanation Sheet" by Robert A. Male, Associate Director, Guidance Institute for Talented Students, University of Wisconsin-Madison, 1979. List of student characteristics and descriptions of five students from *Gifted Children in the Classroom* by E. Paul Torrance; copyright © 1965 by Macmillan Publishing Company, Inc. "Implementing an Identification Program" from *Guidelines for the Identification of the Gifted and Talented*, University of the State of New York, State Education Department, Albany, 1977. Sample items from *Scales for Rating the Behavioral Characteristics of Superior Students* by Renzulli, Smith, White, Callahan, and Hartman (Creative Learning Press, 1977), Figure 2 (page 7) from *A Guidebook for Developing Individualized Educational Programs for Gifted and Talented Students* by Joseph S. Renzulli and Linda H. Smith; copyright © 1979 by Creative Learning Press.

(*Continued on page 143*)

CONTENTS

PREFACE

Characteristics and Identification of Gifted and Talented Students is the first book in NEA's multimedia program *Educating the Gifted and Talented*, which is designed to provide background information, supplementary materials, workshop activities, and discussion questions for (a) individuals who are preparing to work with gifted and talented students, (b) teachers who currently work with classes of gifted and talented students, and (c) teachers who have a few gifted and talented students in their classes. The materials in this program are also intended to help administrators and parents concerned with issues involved in the education of the gifted and talented. While these groups constitute the primary audience, we believe we have also addressed concerns and ideas affecting teaching at all levels.

We bring to this task our own learning experiences which have been filled not only with a careful study of the research that has been conducted in this field by many different researchers over the past sixty years, but also the knowledge gained from working in classrooms at all levels with gifted and highly gifted students. In addition, we have gained other insights into educating the gifted and talented from our work in school districts with supervisors, program developers, principals, and superintendents, as well as in teacher training programs and workshops throughout the United States. As a result of these experiences, we have tried to give life to the theoretical by including numerous specific examples. Another source of learning has come through our encounters with many forms of literature—short stories, novels, poetry, television, and film—which embody the gifted and talented in dramatic and powerful ways. Therefore, we have also included in our discussions and references materials not customarily found in teacher training literature.

In our work with teachers and students we have found extremely helpful the use of yet another approach to understanding—the metaphorical. For example, we may wish to convince someone of the need to design approaches to curriculum which will seriously take into account individual differences in learning styles, ways of processing information, rates of learning, memory, interests, and skills. Rather than speaking directly to the subject, however, we may be more effective if we first examine

7

a handful of many different kinds of seeds (corn, pumpkin, spinach, squash, acorn, avocado) and then ask, "What is needed to make these seeds grow?" In answering this question it soon becomes evident that any responsible farmer would first find out the kind of seeds involved and then be careful to discover the particular soil, nutrients, water, sunlight, heat or cold, spacing, and planting cycle for each type. To provide a bridge between the seeds and our students we ask the question, "Can we dare to cultivate uniqueness in the classroom?" Any number of books which have appeared in recent years point to the rather startling changes that take place when a person becomes sensitized to the environment. Books like *Stalking the Wild Asparagus* (4) and *One Hundred Sixty Edible Plants* (2) are all intent upon sharpening our perceptions of the world around us. Where the untrained eye once looked upon a field and saw a collection of weeds, the same field seen by the trained and practiced eye of the naturalist can yield a virtual bouquet of delights. The field has not changed, but the observer is able to perceive the nature and quality of its contents because of a special training.

If such an approach is new or unusual, we encourage you to consider it as a possible method to explore not only for yourself but also for your working with the gifted.

The general format of this book incorporates both discussion and application of each major topic by a division of the text into three sections. The first section offers background information and ideas on each topic. The second section provides supplementary materials and examples for your interest and use. Finally, the third section presents a series of activities to help you become involved with the topic and to help apply the ideas to your specific situation. Throughout the text we have embedded examples, related experiences, and commentary for interest as well as to illustrate the ideas. (Although the facts in the anecdotes are true, the names of persons involved have been changed to protect their privacy.) This format is intended to help you with background information and, especially, with internalization and application of the various ideas about the major topics.

The first book in this project begins with a discussion of some of the many characteristics of gifted and talented students by focusing on individual abilities, interests, and needs and by encouraging the reader to look closely at specific students. By developing an ever-increasing sensitivity to the presence of these characteristics and the behaviors which reflect them, we as teachers can better enable students to continue to enlarge and expand their horizons. Not only will this increased awareness affect the gifted and talented, but it will also affect other students as we begin to look more positively at some of their divergent behaviors.

Although the various areas of concern are presented in a sequential fashion throughout the different texts, teachers and program developers are encouraged to move freely back and forth among them. While considering program development, for example, specific characteristics of gifted and talented students in the school population should be kept clearly in mind so that the strategies developed will build upon these characteristics rather than contradict them. If, for example, the aim is to design a program to develop general intellectual or creative abilities, it would probably be well to avoid a narrow, accelerated, content-oriented curriculum, the focus of which would be in opposition to the broad interests and probing curiosity characteristic of this population.

We gratefully acknowledge the many substantive contributions to this work by Margot Nicholas Parrot of Hancock, Maine. As a parent of three highly gifted children and as an adult with many gifts herself, Gotte has brought a level of practical insight and fearless and straightforward comment and energy to all her interaction with us.

We are grateful, too, for the comments of the teachers and administrators enrolled in the Gifted Institute taught by Fred Tuttle and Hap Metivier during the spring of 1979, as well as for the comments of those teachers who worked with these materials in the fall of 1979.

Special thanks are also extended to Patricia Tuttle and Rosanne Becker for their extreme patience and endurance during the many writing sessions involved in the completion of this work.

INTRODUCTION
TO THE
SECOND EDITION

Many people believe that only those directly involved with programs for gifted and talented students need to be concerned about their characteristics or about methods of identifying them. To be sure, those who are directly involved have a special concern for gifted students and such knowledge is indeed vital to developing and implementing a successful program. It may be even more important, however, for teachers and administrators who are not directly involved in the formal education of gifted students to become well acquainted with their characteristics and the procedures for identifying them. All teachers work with gifted students, whether or not they have a "gifted class." Even special education teachers work with gifted students who may have specific learning disabilities or emotional difficulties. The need to know about the gifted pervades all levels of education.

One thread underlies nearly all goals of education: to provide quality education based on individual needs and abilities. This of course has been the rallying cry for the development of all special programs. It is also the obligation of all teachers, whether in special programs or in general classrooms. To meet this obligation teachers must first be aware of the various needs of their students. Consequently, they should know the characteristics of the gifted and how those qualities affect learning.

This edition of *Characteristics and Identification of Gifted and Talented Students* includes more examples of various types of gifted students and stresses some of the characteristics that teachers are likely to encounter in classroom situations. It also provides a variety of forms and checklists used by educators to locate gifted students both in individual classrooms and throughout school systems. While formal identification of gifted students may not be vital in a particular class, awareness of the characteristics and of the methods of locating the individuals who possess them is important if teachers are to meet each student's needs.

CHARACTERISTICS

Bill is a good kid. He does not work very hard in class but, then again, he doesn't have to in order to pass. However, he really frustrates his teachers. They know he could do much better than he does. When he studies, which is seldom, he scores at the top of the scale. Even without studying he performs well enough to pass easily. He seems to go out of his way to avoid work and then to create excuses for not having it done. If he put as much effort into doing his work as he does into not doing it, he would be at the top of his class. As one teacher said, "I really enjoy talking with Bill outside class, but in class he is very difficult. I just can't get him to do the work and he constantly leads the discussion off on tangents. Even the other kids are beginning to tire of his digressions and excuses."

Jane sits quietly in the front of the class. She does all her work on time and perfectly within the parameters of the assignment. Always in the top two or three on class tests, Jane is a joy to have in class. I just wish more students would cooperate as she does.

Mary used to be one of the best math students in school. She still scores in the top five per cent on math aptitude tests; but ever since eighth grade she seems to have lost all interest in math and math-related areas. She is very popular and does her work adequately but it seems as if she could do so much better.

Jim is different from any student I have ever had in class. I can't tell if he is serious about his answers or is just joking, trying to test my reaction. I cannot always take time in class to ask him to explain his answers, but when I do question him after class, his answers make sense. Lately, however, he has stopped participating and just sits there quietly, sometimes making comments about what I or other students say. This is beginning to bother me and some of his classmates.

These comments from teachers reflect only a few of those often made about gifted individuals in the classroom. While the comments sometimes reflect teachers' frustrations, they also indicate the initial recognition of the problem. In too many classes the characteristics and behaviors of these students are viewed only as discipline or behavior problems. Many of us recognize only "Mary" as gifted, placing the others into different categories. By the nature of most academic situations, the behaviors that conform to teacher expectations are highly rewarded while those that do not conform are usually penalized when noticed.

INDICATORS OF GIFTEDNESS

Gifted and talented individuals are many times stereotyped as being emotionally tense, high-strung, uncoordinated, and bookish. This description as misfits has been disproved repeatedly by many educators and researchers who have found that often the gifted are the social as well as the intellectual leaders. As Gallagher states, the gifted are "almost invariably more popular and more socially accepted than children at other levels of intellectual ability." (3) In many situations the gifted individual may be the class leader rather than the class oddity—depending, of course, on the specific school and the values of teachers and students, and whether the particular type of abilities are held in high esteem. The degree of ability may also affect the leadership role. Einstein and Churchill were hardly class presidents.

The "class leader" in Edward's class is, in fact, gifted both intellectually and in sports. However, he is not so far ahead of his classmates academically as Edward is, and this may make a difference in terms of general social leadership. Edward, a third grader, seems to be better accepted in his fifth grade math class.

The term *gifted* has been greatly expanded since the early researchers like Terman began their studies. Torrance, Gowan, Guilford, Taylor and many others, for example, have continually stressed skills and talents other than academic ability and IQ, emphasizing areas such as creative thinking and problem solving. (See also *Issues in Gifted Education* (3a) and *What Makes Giftedness* (10a).) To reflect this expanding concept of giftedness, the U.S. Office of Education reports of 1972 and 1978 broadened the definition of gifted and talented to include several areas beyond intellectual and academic abilities. (See "Problems of Definition.")

Several lists of characteristics of gifted individuals have been disseminated throughout the country. (See Supplementary Materials.) Regardless of list selected, it should be remembered that the behaviors cited merely give tentative, general characteristics. Particular gifted individuals may not possess all the characteristics and may indeed act in such a way to conceal these traits, especially as they progress through school. If the school allows and encourages individuals to exhibit their natural traits, however, certain characteristics will become more evident.

Typical of such lists of characteristics reflecting gifted ability is the following:

A gifted individual—
1. is curious.
2. is persistent in pursuit of interests and questions.
3. is perceptive of the environment.
4. is critical of self and others.
5. has a highly developed sense of humor, often a verbal orientation.
6. is sensitive to injustices on personal and worldwide levels.
7. is a leader in various areas.
8. is not willing to accept superficial statements, responses, or evaluations.
9. understands general principles easily.
10. often responds to the environment through media and means other than print and writing.
11. sees relationships among seemingly diverse ideas.
12. generates many ideas for a specific stimulus.

The foregoing characteristics may be grouped into three areas: personal (1–3), interpersonal (4–7), and processing of information (8–12). Another perspective is suggested by Donald Nasca, State University of New York, College at Brockport, who has described gifted learners using computer terminology: "If you take a look at the number of descriptors that we can put together on giftedness, they comprise three different categories. First of all, is sensory input. Gifted students are capable of receiving more information from their environment. Secondly, is storage capacity. They are able to store more information. Third, is processing of information. Gifted students seem to be able to call upon a greater variety of techniques to process information that they have available. The gifted are producers of information whereas their age-mates tend to be accumulators of information and recallers of information." (15)

Although these lists describe behaviors which the gifted may exhibit in a classroom, sometimes the characteristics of gifted individuals become evident even before school age. When viewing indicative behaviors of preschool children, we should ask ourselves if the behaviors are different from those expected of other children of the same age. Margot Parrot, a parent of three highly gifted children, shared the following characteristics and indicative behaviors of preschool gifted children from her own experiences and extensive readings as a concerned parent.

1. Early language acquisition: uses a large vocabulary; speaks in long, complex sentences; talks early and often. Many gifted children, however, do not speak early but wait until they are older and then display a remarkable facility with language.

2. Fine and gross motor skills: walks, climbs, runs early and well; controls small objects such as scissors, pencils, crayons, etc., easily; copies pictures and words; handles tools well.

3. Intellectual areas: reads signs or even books; does mathematical problems; draws associations among diverse ideas; remembers facts and events; is interested in social and moral issues; has a long attention span; asks why.

4. Social areas: has empathy for others; is self-confident and independent; organizes and leads group activities; very active both mentally and physically.

5. Creative areas: has a vivid imagination; enjoys playing with words and ideas; shows a highly developed, often verbal sense of humor; uses objects, toys, colors in imaginative ways.

6. Specific areas: plays musical instrument; plays sports well; sings; in general, shows remarkable ability in specific area.

According to Parrot, "In identifying by traits, it all boils down to being different, either in kind or intensity."

If your initial reaction to this list is to wonder how it differs from other lists, perhaps you share the viewpoint favored by Halbert B. Robinson, Director of the Center for Study of Gifted Children, University of Washington, Seattle, who states: "I know of no evidence, however, that gifted children are in any meaningful way different than other children. They are precocious, we know, but precocity has more to say about their rate of development in the area of their gifts than about the qualitative path their development has taken." (11)

I've been thinking about what exactly made my children so different, from an early age. With Edward it was: *motivation* (he went from a helpless infant to a child who could crawl, sit, stand, walk holding on, and even *speak*; early *speech* (putting two words together at nine months when most babies don't even *know* two words); memory, sensitivity to environment and to other people; and *piercing questions*. Then, of course, there was his early reading (books at four and one-half) and mathematical ability (by five and one-half he had mastered all major concepts of elementary school math in his head). Chrysal was entirely different. Her motor ability and verbal ability developed earlier but over a longer period (at two and one-half to three months, Chrysal devised a means of locomotion: she would roll across the floor to get to a desired object), by two she had mastered scissors completely. At three she was writing legibly and doing art work which was identifiable. From three to five she was too ill to show her remarkable mental abilities, so I was surprised to learn how high her IQ was. She read at about four and one-half to five. Her emotional development was moderately impaired by illness—her own illness and her baby brother's. Louis' *memory* was amazing as a baby—and from the time he was an infant he seemed to be *unusually friendly and well adjusted*—which was more amazing considering the fact that he spent much of his babyhood in the hospital—often either in pain or drugged and much of his toddlerhood in isolation to prevent infection. He is, at three, not only very *verbal and perceptive*, but also very outgoing and secure. He loves classical music and sings well. *He plays with words and ideas like toys.* His understanding of math concepts is becoming more obvious and although he has been reading some words since two, he is just starting to put together the skills to read phonically. I expect him to read at a first grade level in a few more months, at age four.

The thing that I realize upon looking back is that all three children were showing evidence of giftedness before the age of one year old and all three were branching out into areas in which they would excel by age two. By that time, strangers would make such remarks as "Isn't he the smart one," or "He seems more like three than two." I suppose I agree with Robinson that precocity is the main thing. But these kids have a way of interacting with their environment that does seem *qualitatively* different—call it deeper perception, perhaps. My kids seem to do some things that most other kids *just don't do* at any age. (This difference may be cultural, though.) The difference between mental age, emotional age, and physical age (at one point Chrysal was "classified" as having a mental age of nine and one-half, emotional age of two to four, and physical age of five and one-half) seems to produce unique characteristics, besides. When a child in diapers is reading, I for one am curious about how he views the world.

(Margot Parrot)

These lists of characteristics of gifted and talented individuals are usually appropriate for the majority of our populations. Many of these behaviors, however, may not reflect giftedness in individuals from different cultural backgrounds and environments. An example from one group, First Americans, will illustrate this caution.

In this culture, or variety of cultures, many of the indicators of superior abilities may be in opposition to those most often found on lists of characteristics of gifted and talented—high verbal ability, impatience, and persistence in pursuit of answers. For many First Americans, such behaviors conflict with their cultural expectations and would not therefore be evidenced by gifted individuals in that population.

Examining work done by E. P. Torrance (14), Tom Peacock, Director of Education for the Minnesota Chippewa Tribe, comments on the characteristics listed by Torrance in relation to the Chippewa Tribe:

- *Emotional Responsiveness*—What the psychologist Alan Briskin would refer to as emotional excitability. This type of person listens intensely and has a strong empathy for others—is highly aware of the feelings, distress, and needs of others.
- *Richness of Imagery*—The Chippewa language is rich in imagery. This type of student shows strong imagery in dance, movement, in relating to experiences, in oral reading, in role-playing, and dramatics and drawing and other art work.
- *Responsiveness to the Concrete*—This may be an adaptive response to poverty and discrimination. The natural response to these may be a pride in strength and distrust of schooling.
- *Enjoyment of and Ability in Creative Movement and Dance*—This type of student experiences deep enjoyment in creative movement and dance and becomes deeply absorbed in it. Such students are excellent interpreters of movement and dance. In the Indian world this is easily noticed in the dance of our talented traditional and fancy dancers.
- *Enjoyment and Ability in Visual Arts*—This student experiences real joy in drawing, painting, sculpture, or photography and becomes deeply absorbed in it. Some of these students go to the Institute for American Indian Arts if their ability is recognized and nurtured. The beauty of

16

Indian crafts leads one to believe we have many gifted artists.

- *Ability to Improvise with Commonplace Materials and Objects*—Indian children who have grown up in poverty exhibit this trait in a sometimes humorous manner. One Tribal Chairman reflected to me how after Christmas in his school the teacher would have show and tell so the students could bring their favorite Christmas present. He said his toys were kettles and silverware, and he used raw potatoes as his toy trucks and cars. A sad case in point, but I once observed a child using a beer can as a car and making motor sounds—doing circle spins. Sometimes it is an adaptive response to not having any toys or games. Students may exhibit this behavior by making toys and games from commonplace things, using common materials for unintended uses at home and school, and using common material inventions. (8)

Although the lists of characteristics of gifted and talented ability provide valuable tools for locating and identifying these individuals in schools, several cautions about their implementation are suggested. *First*, the lists reflect several traits, and specific indicators should be developed to reflect particular situations and types of giftedness. *Second*, these characteristics will be demonstrated only in environments which encourage individuals to display them. *Third*, individuals within different cultures may have characteristics not included on general lists or which may even be in opposition to those usually cited. Consequently, the search for indicators of giftedness should take into account the total environment, of both giftedness and the population, before the most appropriate decision for a particular school is made.

PROBLEMS ENCOUNTERED BY GIFTED

Too often the behaviors indicative of superior abilities create difficulties for the gifted individual.

Even with an extensive list of characteristics, it is difficult to determine giftedness in many students who have learned, consciously or subconsciously, to hide their true abilities. This statement may sound strange, but it is not when we examine the conditions under which the gifted have to function. First, their peers may place little value on intellectual giftedness. The athlete is admired and the clown is honored, but the intellectual is often ridiculed by classmates. Consider the case of the student

17

who wrote a letter to an editor asking if it would be immoral to cheat on tests to achieve a lower score. This girl scored so well on her exams that she was affecting the curve, causing her classmates to receive lower grades. Michael Pyryt conducted a study in 1976 on the perceptions of inner-city youths toward the gifted. He found that "The inner-city students saw the mathematically talented students as show offs while the gifted students themselves and their teachers saw them as more argumentative and opinionated." (9)

Cecelia Solano noted in 1976 that "students from a more middle-class school also saw the gifted as conceited and boastful." (13) As a result of peer pressure, and perhaps even teacher pressure, many gifted students become withdrawn or rebellious in the classroom, making it even more difficult to recognize their true potential.

Tara Stuart of Horizons Unlimited, in Keene, New Hampshire, relates a story which illustrates how a gifted individual may be affected by the attitude of peers and teachers.

In England several years ago I recall meeting Neil, a very sensitive and highly gifted child. The advent of kindergarten and first grade provided the trauma of a precocious, joyous child that read at four and played chess at five into a self-effacing, nonverbal seven year old. In attempting to reassure and help her son, Neil's mother one day talked with him about the map of the world and how explorers had traveled across thousands of miles and unknown seas and continents to discover new lands and that when they returned to their own lands, few people could understand and identify with the explorers' new knowledge of the world and all they had undergone to attain it. Then she drew a map to represent the conscious being. She carefully pointed out that in his life he had the capacity to explore the areas of the higher unconscious that many people only glimpsed occasionally, that he was like an explorer. He was exploring the dimensions of his inner world. The bright-eyed Neil burst out, "I wish you had told me that when I was four. I always knew I was different, but I thought I was different in a bad sort of way." (15)

To avoid creating similar feelings in other children, we should learn to observe students individually with the expectation that perhaps their behavior might be indicative of potential superior ability. The following discussion focuses attention on characteristics and behaviors which are accepted as potential indications of giftedness but which often create problems in traditional academic settings.

Divergent and Associative Thinking

By "divergent" we usually mean behaviors outside the norm, doing things in unusual ways and arriving at different solutions. A divergent thinker may have apparently erroneous answers but, when asked to explain such answers, can usually prove the "wrong answer" is valid if looked at from another point of view. Most teachers, however, have too much content to cover, too many students, and too little time to allow such students to demonstrate the validity of the divergent response and may tend to mark these responses incorrect. As a result the student may accept the teacher's opinion without question and begin to doubt his or her own thinking processes.

Part of divergent thinking is related to the ability to draw associations among several seemingly disparate ideas. Sometimes this ability leads individuals to paths not usually followed by peers or even by teachers, affecting not only the types of responses they may give, but also their perception of tasks. For example, a commonly stated characteristic of giftedness is the ability to accomplish tasks quickly. This is not always true, however.

Hannah's third grade teacher asked students to think about the word "blue" for homework and be prepared to list some things they associate with it. The teacher thought it would be a five- or ten-minute task, since all she wanted was a list of items commonly colored blue (e.g., sky, boy's baby blanket). For Hannah, however, the assignment took nearly two hours since she began to explore "blue" as it related to the army of the North in the Civil War, the emotion of being "blue," and the color itself in a variety of ways.

The desire to delve into a subject, exploring the variety of associations envisioned, may make a seemingly short, simple assignment very complicated and time-consuming for these individuals. Some may even rebel in the classroom setting and achieve the questionable status of troublemaker.

Critical Thinking

Gifted individuals are sometimes critical of others as well as of themselves. This trait can also create problems for them. Often they have a desire for more in-depth answers to questions and more extensive exploration of issues than is possible in most traditional classrooms. When this desire is not fulfilled, they may react critically toward those responding. Their reaction, either with a verbal side comment or a nonverbal facial expression, sometimes alienates gifted students from either the teacher or

19

the peers for whom the answer is sufficient. In such situations all are frustrated. The gifted are frustrated because their curiosity has not been satisfied. Teachers are frustrated because they would like to spend more time on the topic but know the other students would rapidly lose interest. And classmates are frustrated because they feel criticized by the gifted. When gifted students become defensive about their reactions, they sometimes extend their critical comments, increasing the frustration and potential for antagonistic relationships.

Self-criticism may also create difficulties for the gifted, especially when it becomes too strong. Sometimes this problem begins early in life. When very young, many gifted persons are able to do many things extremely well. Their parents, in turn, usually praise them for their accomplishments. While certainly an appropriate response, continual praise and increasing expectations may inadvertently help an individual become very self-critical. In later years this self-criticism may take several forms— for example, refusing to attempt any task about which the person feels any insecurity or chance of failure. Some teachers find such students continually turning in work late, believing it is not good enough to turn in "yet." Obviously, these responses to self-criticism can endanger their success in the classroom. Unrealistic self-expectations and too strong a desire to be "perfect" in all things at all times can lead the critical nature to create some emotional problems for the gifted not faced by many other individuals.

Jeff was a very good student but he seemed unable to submit papers on time. For example, one paper was a week late because he had to "get it right" before submitting it. Then he felt he should make it better to compensate for the tardiness. When it was two weeks late, Jeff decided it had to be even better, making it three weeks late. Finally the teacher asked him to turn it in as is. Jeff sensed that somehow he had to balance quality and quantity and still meet the "deadline" while remaining satisfied with the effort and the product. Because of his own high standards, the task was not a simple matter of dashing it off and handing it in, as it was for some other students.

Organizing material may also present problems for the gifted in the classroom. For most of us the traditional pattern of organizing notes and references is helpful because we may have difficulty keeping track of ideas in the absence of an observable system of organization. The gifted individual, on the other hand, often establishes a unique pattern of organization that makes sense only to that person, if it makes sense at all. To an observer the arrangement appears as disorganization. This "creative clutter," however, is necessary for that person, as the various associations among the seemingly different items are an integral part of the organization.

Rose's desk is a mess by most standards. However, everything fits into an elaborate individual filing system; for whenever she wants a note card, book, or reference, Rose can reach into this clutter and produce it immediately. It may not fit the teacher's idea or method of organization, but it works for Rose. Whenever she is forced to "clean it up," she loses track of things for days.

In some classrooms such highly individual arrangements of materials can create problems if the gifted individual is forced to follow the same "tried and true" method of organization as everyone else or is marked down accordingly. Once again the assumption behind such attitudes and practices may be that someone else, "an expert," knows better than the individual student what is "best" for the student. The process of self-discovery which results from the individual's direct experience is denied as the acceptance of authority is reinforced. To be sure, with some gifted children the "creative clutter" is nothing more than a mess. These students can profit by examining several methods of organization and selecting or developing the one best suited to their personalities and purposes.

Variety of Valid Alternatives

Charles Pulvino of the University of Wisconsin has observed that one of the major problems confronting gifted individuals in high school is that of choice. For most of us the areas in which we may focus our future efforts are limited since our talents and energies allow us to excel in only one or two fields. For the gifted individual, however, many more paths are open as the potential for superior achievement in any of them is real. While many may consider this situation a benefit, it often creates problems because of the variety of pressures to select a single path early in one's career. Faced with pressures from many fronts (from society to contribute to the welfare of all, from academia to excel on a theoretical level, from parents and peers to advance financially, and from self to achieve satisfaction), gifted individuals often find themselves in a dilemma which creates severe internal conflicts.

In this age of specialization, contemporary society does not place a high value on the Renaissance individual, one who excels at many tasks and specializes in more than one throughout a lifetime. The individual who selects an occupation early and stays with it until retirement tends to be rewarded. The individual who moves from one job to another may be viewed as "shiftless" and may have to begin rebuilding financial security with each move. The short poem "Curiosity" by Alistair Reid (10) embodies some of the societal attitudes toward these "wandering" and "irresponsible" but curious individuals and provides a hint as to why they behave as they do.

Occasionally, when the gifted are forced to limit their scope and live within the confines of a narrow selection of alternatives, they are made to feel unacceptable as persons. This is particularly true of individuals in groups for which society holds role expectations. Gifted girls within our culture, for example, are especially susceptible to such pressure.

Maria has always had a variety of paths open to her but has faced continual internal conflicts because of these alternatives. As a youth she was selected for a special university program for students gifted in creative writing. At fifteen she was chosen to join the opera workshop at a nearby college and consequently received a scholarship for voice. Her family felt this was not a wise decision financially, however, so Maria went to a technological institute where she excelled as an engineering student. This field was also thwarted when her counselor advised her against pursuing engineering, as the field was closed to women and there was already a surplus of engineers. From there Maria went to a state university where she majored in general education with a minor in premed. Again she excelled in several areas, especially biology and eugenics. Now, many avenues were open to her. Unable to settle on any one, she married, postponing decisions about her own career, which left her with deep feelings of lack of fulfillment. She therefore began to work in education, with special emphasis in psychotherapy. Within this general field she has moved several times. In addition, she has become particularly adept in carpentry, cabinetry, painting, ceramics, sewing, and writing. Even with the career in education guaranteed, however, Maria has felt frustration because of a belief that she is obligated to work only in education; and she has felt guilty about moving or even considering moving into other areas in which she is equally gifted.

Diverse Responses

Not only are gifted individuals able to perceive a great deal of their environment and to draw from it a wide variety of associations, they are also able to express their perceptions and understandings to others in a wide variety of ways. Most schools accept only one mode of response: print. As a rule high academic value is not placed on film, dance, art, or drama as expressions of understanding of concepts. Test-taking and essay-writing may provide teachers with the bulk of their perceptions of student ability. The student may be allowed to express ideas and feelings through another medium such as film, but ultimately the student is required to respond in print in order to receive adequate evaluation and subsequent academic approval. A course which allows the use of nonprint material for evaluation would not often be considered a "solid," academic course. Gifted students who may find other media more appropriate for presentations of their understandings are therefore penalized by the academic world.

Emily, a tenth grader who was particularly interested in mime, asked if she could do a special, self-initiated study of it as part of her work in English class. The teacher granted her request. While the rest of the class was reading *Macbeth*, Emily studied mime, not to avoid reading the play but as a positive alternative to it. After extensive reading and research, Emily went to a nearby elementary school where she taught mime to the children. The teacher gave her credit for her work, but he received considerable criticism from the rest of the faculty because Emily had not taken the test on *Macbeth*. Instead, she had performed in the elementary school, worked with the children, and documented the experience on slides and film.

Persistence

A major objective of most teachers is to motivate students to pursue academic goals. This objective is reflected in the 1978–79 National Council of Teachers of English publication *Classroom Practices in Teaching English*, subtitled *Activating the Passive Student*. Usually the effort to provide motivation extends for several weeks until the unit is complete and then teachers move to another topic. Teachers whose classes contain gifted and talented learners might perhaps perceive the problem as how to deactivate these students rather than to activate them. Once a gifted individual becomes involved in a particular area, interest and singular pursuit of knowledge in that area are often long-lived. It has also been the authors' experience that once a person becomes convinced that learning is his/her own responsibility, a teacher would not dare assign the amount of work voluntarily attempted by that learner. While initially quite gratifying, such persistence may frustrate the teacher who wants the individual to stay with the class and become equally involved in other units. When teacher frustration becomes too great, the student is persuaded to abandon the topic and follow the rest of the class.

Another area in which persistence may cause problems for the gifted individual is in the daily class discussion. In most such instances, specific answers to questions are expected and a limited amount of time is available for digressions from the expected answers. Gifted individuals, however, have the ability to see beyond the superficial answers and often want to move the discussion to these other areas. Often such behavior may be viewed as disruptive because it detracts from the intended line of questioning.

> I stopped asking questions in my calculus class since I obviously annoyed the professor. I kept seeing new connections that he hadn't explained and didn't intend to. The nonmath lovers resented my questions, too, since they didn't want to be further confused.

Even the gifted student's direct answer may cause problems, as the student may have a special insight or additional knowledge which produces an alternative answer to the one wanted and expected. Most teachers will allow the individual to state the alternative answer, but few will permit the persistent delving into the alternate route because class time will not accommodate such digression and few other students will be able to follow the discussion. The teacher, too, may be unable to follow the direction suggested by the digression. Such a situation may also pose a significant threat to the self-confidence of the teacher. Once again, the gifted individual is frustrated and penalized for the very characteristics that indicate exceptional ability.

Further, intellectually gifted students may be perceived as rude or obnoxious because of their persistence and tenacity—the line between persistence and insubordination being sometimes difficult to determine. It is well to keep in mind, however, that rudeness is a description of the way certain behaviors are perceived by a specific observer, which involves a value judgment about those behaviors. Such judgment often has serious implications for the relationship between the observer and the person whose behavior has been labeled rude. By examining these characteristics, it is hoped that it will be realized that actions may reflect attitudes other than the superficial ones—that obnoxious behavior, for example, may actually stem from a real interest in an area, not from a desire to irritate or anger.

These and other problem-creating characteristics of gifted individuals may result in even more serious negative classroom behaviors, including antisocial acting out to achieve recognition; intentional failure to gain attention or to mask ability; deliberately careless or messy work; and an active distrust of teachers and other adults. This is certainly not to imply that all students who display unacceptable behaviors are necessarily gifted; or that all gifted students display these behaviors or have the described difficulties. Rather, it is vital to look beyond the surface manifestation of the behavior to the underlying causes. When seeking to find out why a student is bored, withdrawn, uncooperative, rebellious, teachers may find the cause related to the individual's particular learning characteristics, such as advanced divergent, associative, and critical thinking skills. An inability to address these learning needs may promote the various reactions from students. If the negative behaviors are prolonged, they may cause additional problems in the future. For example, lack of challenging work in early grades may give rise to a careless attitude toward work and, in time, to an inability to perform to capacity when work becomes more challenging.

Jack is content with slightly above-average grades with very little effort. Usually he begins and completes a project the night before it is due or studies for exams during the preceding class. This approach has been successful as he usually receives A's or B's for these efforts. Now, however, faced with more difficult classes, he is unable to adapt his time to prepare adequately for tests and projects. Not only are his grades dropping drastically, but he is losing confidence in himself and becoming frustrated by the situation.

The feelings of rejection by peers and teachers sometimes create severe emotional problems in gifted individuals. When unable to achieve their potential in school, they may seek other outlets, some of which may be quite unacceptable to both school and society.

In the short story "The Substitute," Zenna Henderson (5) depicts a situation in which Keely, a disruptive student, continually antagonizes teachers and refuses to perform the tasks demanded of the class. The conflict is resolved when a "substitute" teacher recognizes that the gum and wires which cluttered his desk were really a sophisticated radio which permitted him to converse with extraterrestrial beings.

By focusing attention on individual behavior as a potential indication of gifted ability, we may be able to reexamine the rebellious student, the "far-out" student, the withdrawn student, the hyperactive student, and the daydreamer.

Awareness of the characteristics reflected by these behaviors is essential for program development. To design an appropriate program for any group of students, we must know their particular learning characteristics so that the program may meet their special needs and interests. Knowledge of characteristics and indicative behaviors first enables us to recognize individuals with particular needs and then to provide vital learning environments to accommodate and build upon these traits.

A few years ago I was asked to visit a first grade classroom to observe Jan, a student who was causing both parents and teacher considerable frustration. When I entered the class, Jan was sitting in the left rear corner of the room with his daily work piled in front of him. Instead of paying attention to either the work or the teacher, he was focusing all his efforts on throwing a pencil into the air and catching it. Taking Jan and his papers into another room, I asked him first to do all the math problems on one worksheet on the two diagonals. Without asking for the definition of "diagonal," Jan immediately completed the specified items without error. Then I asked him to perform similar tasks with the other worksheets.

After he completed these tasks, also without error, I asked this first grader if he enjoyed reading. When he indicated that he did, especially reading about dinosaurs, I told him to go to the card catalogue in the library, look up "dinosaur," select a book, and bring it back to the room. He did so without difficulty and began to read. After he completed the reading, I asked him several questions to be sure that his faultless oral reading was not just the result of a good phonics background. It was not. He demonstrated complete comprehension of this randomly selected book on dinosaurs which would have posed problems for most fifth graders.

When I asked Jan why he refused to do the work in class, especially since it was so obvious that he could do it easily, he replied, "I am just not learning anything from it." He was not referring to the skills but rather to the often meaningless content used to teach the various skills, particularly the phonics lessons. Most young students complete work even when they do not see the reason for it. Gifted individuals, however, sometimes rebel. Since I was also working with some gifted sixth graders at the time, I asked one of my students who was interested in teaching to develop some phonics lessons for Jan, focusing on the skills stressed by the first grade teacher but using dinosaur as the underlying vehicle for the lessons. Although Jan enjoyed this work and completed all the tasks, he still had difficulty passing first grade because his teacher felt he was "irresponsible" and consequently should not go to second grade until he completed all work assigned in her class.

26

PROBLEMS OF DEFINITION

It is a mistake to become overly concerned with the definition of the gifted and talented until you have some idea of resources, program goals, and population with which you might work. At this point it is sufficient to establish a general definition and then refine it as the program develops.

In 1978, Congress passed a bill which among other things updated the definition of gifted and talented students. The revised definition stated in Public Law 95–561 of November 1, 1978, reads:

For the purpose of this part, the term gifted and talented children means children and, whenever applicable, youth, who are identified at the preschool, elementary, or secondary level as possessing demonstrated or potential abilities that give evidence of high performance in capability in areas such as intellectual, creative, specific academic, or leadership ability, or in the performing and visual arts, and who by reason thereof require service or activities not ordinarily provided by the school.

This definition is a revision of the one presented in the U.S. Office of Education Report of 1972 in which six general areas for gifted and talented abilities were delineated. The earlier report suggested that a person who possesses superior ability in any of these general categories, either singly or in any combination, should be considered gifted. (1) The list offers teachers and administrators the following six areas of giftedness to explore in developing a program:

General Intellectual Ability. This category includes individuals who demonstrate characteristics such as intellectual curiosity, exceptional powers of observation, ability to abstract, a questioning attitude, and associative thinking skills.

Academic Talent. This area encompasses the excellent students, those who achieve high grades, who score very well on tests, and who demonstrate high ability in academic pursuits. Of course, some of these gifted students do not perform well in school but develop their academic skills outside school. Many schools have already developed programs for the academically gifted, including honors classes and advanced placement courses.

Creative and Productive Thinking Skills. Students with these abilities are often those who come up with original and divergent ideas. In addition, they have the ability to elaborate and develop their original ideas, as well as to realize many different ways of perceiving a single thought or topic. Such students are often overlooked in classrooms where emphasis is on assimilating a quantity of information and repeating predetermined answers.

Leadership. While many educators discuss this ability, few have actually been able to describe it adequately for classroom use. On the one hand, it includes those students who emerge as social or academic leaders in a group. However, leadership should also encompass another trait: the willingness to accept responsibility for one's actions and to have a feeling of control over one's life and decisions. In most programs for gifted students we have found the second trait, personal leadership, to be the more important of the two. Leadership involves use of power, productive interaction with others, and self-control.

Visual and Performing Arts. This area relates to activities such as painting, sculpting, drawing, filmmaking, dancing, singing, playing instruments, and performing dramatically. Individuals with superior abilities in these fields seldom have the opportunity to demonstrate their giftedness in most academic classes as the behaviors which reflect such abilities are usually relegated to outside-of-class work and then encouraged only if academic requirements have been fulfilled. Currently, however, some educators and programs, such as the Education Center for the Arts in New Haven (Connecticut) and the Houston (Texas) School for the Visual and Performing Arts, are stressing this area of giftedness.

Psychomotor Skills. Although this category was not specifically referred to in the 1978 definition, the earlier report recognized its importance. We also believe it is an area worthy of special mention. Besides encompassing athletic prowess, as reflected in many sports programs, it includes superior use of fine motor skills as found in exceptional woodworking, crafts, drafting, and mechanical abilities. In most schools these abilities are usually developed under vocational education where superior performances by students in these areas are seldom acknowledged as gifted. In fact, referral to such programs is often considered a viable option for somewhat disabled learners. An exception to this practice is the woodworking program at the Hill School in Pottstown, Pennsylvania. (7)

The foregoing list gives a broad view of areas where gifted individuals may be sought out and helped to develop their abilities. It would be a mistake, however, to accept this list as the definition of gifted and talented for a particular program. Such a definition should evolve from a discussion of the goals of the program and the characteristics of the specific population for which the program is designed.

While we tend to use the terms "gifted" and "talented" as one area of abilities, some teachers raise the question about the distinction between giftedness and talent. Both, indeed, reflect superior abilities. However, some have differentiated between these two terms. Virginia Erlich, for example, has made the following delineation:

> By giftedness we mean intellectual prowess such as is evidenced by scores on conventional intelligence tests, and which is characterized by an ability to see and group relationships, proficiency in verbal abstract thought, persistence, intellectual curiosity, versatility and adaptability and creative thought.
>
> By talent we mean any specialized skill or ability in a particular field of endeavor, such as the creative and performing arts or sports, where the behavior involves some physical component of muscular coordination, visual acuity, manual dexterity, etc. (1)

Ann Lamkins separates the concept of gifted into three categories: gifted, talented, and potentially gifted.

> Gifted students are those who are consistently able to apply their highly developed skills and knowledge, as well as their personal characteristics, to creative problem-finding/solving in a particular area of human endeavor such as academics, the visual/performing arts, or psychomotor activities. The accomplishments of the gifted are possible because they have exceptional aptitude for achievement in one or more areas of human endeavor and are able to develop them fully

because of personal characteristics. They also apply themselves to the development and completion of their creative ideas. They may be referred to as "outstanding," "exceptional," or "very creative" students, because of the quality and consistency of their performances and products.

Talented students are those who consistently demonstrate high performance with fundamental skills and knowledge as well as personal characteristics. Teachers usually enjoy these students. They like school, are very cooperative, practice their lessons, and do their assignments. They can assimilate and reproduce complex ideas and concepts, but *they do not create their own*. In other words, they are primarily consumers and transmitters of knowledge. The accomplishments of talented children are possible because they are able to apply their personal characteristics to the development of aptitudes. The *academically* talented are often referred to as "bright," "very capable," "excellent students," or "high achievers," and score at or above the 90th percentile on achievement tests in a particular area. They may or may not score exceptionally high on intelligence measures.

Students who show potential for functioning at high levels of performance in . . . fundamental skills and knowledge and . . . creative problem-finding/solving skills, but express personal growth characteristics in the school setting in negative ways, have potential which lies in the development of psychosocial factors. The school setting, including teachers' attitudes, values, and instructional methodologies must be carefully examined and perhaps modified if this type of potentially gifted student is to be identified and programmed. (6)

Embedded in these distinctions and definitions are several different philosophies and attitudes toward the gifted and toward ways of meeting their needs. While all such definitions offer a great deal for discussion, teachers or school systems should not accept any of them without first examining their own unique situations and philosophies.

In this work the term "gifted" is used to refer to both the gifted and the talented, if such a distinction does indeed exist. Periodically, both terms are used to reinforce the inclusion of all these individuals with superior abilities. In addition, we believe that the separation between the gifted and the nongifted is not a clearly defined line. Rather, there is a continuum of abilities and the "breakoff" point between gifted and nongifted is very nebulous—so nebulous, in fact, that many "nongifted" individuals cross into the gifted range intermittently in particular areas when their interests are sufficiently aroused.

For this reason, program developers and teachers are cautioned against too rigid a cutoff point or too narrow a definition of gifted. As the program develops and the population becomes more focused, a definition which describes the particular students for the program may be formulated. If a committee becomes too concerned with a precise definition at the outset of program development, a great deal of time may be spent on discussions which may not have any relevance to the program once some of the realities are observed. For example, if a committee decides to define as gifted those individuals who show exceptional ability in dance and then finds very little support and few resources in the community for such activities, the definition will have to be modified anyway. Developers should have a general understanding of gifted and talented, and gather information about the values and goals of the community before defining "gifted." Then, as the components of the program develop, an accurate, meaningful definition may be derived.

Once we acquire a general understanding of the characteristics and needs of gifted students, we can explore the resources available and some of the parameters within which to work. Then we can more clearly define the gifted population to be identified. It is important to have these understandings before designing an identification procedure because the relationship among the characteristics, the identification procedure, and program must be clear. Otherwise there is a strong possibility that the procedure will identify the wrong population for the program.

In one of my graduate courses in gifted education, a teacher described a problem with the program in her school. Students were identified for the program by teacher referrals based on academic and classroom performance and standardized reading test results. The program, however, focused on instruction in creative art. Unhappy and frustrated, many students dropped out in the first year. Academically talented students had been identified for a program designed for creative individuals. While some of the students belonged in both areas, many of those identified did not belong in the program, and those who should have been in the program had been completely overlooked.

References

1. *Education of the Gifted and Talented: Report to the Congress of the United States by the U.S. Commissioner of Education. U.S. Department of Health, Education and Welfare, Office of Education.* Washington, D.C.: Government Printing Office, 1972.
2. Freitus, Joe. *One Hundred Sixty Edible Plants.* Lexington, Mass.: Stone Wall Press, 1975.
3. Gallagher, James J. *Research Summary on Gifted Child Education.* State of Illinois: Office of the Superintendent of Public Instruction, 1966.
3a. _____; Gowan, J. C.; Passow, A. H.; and Torrance, E. P. *Issues in Gifted Education.* Los Angeles: N/S-LTI-G/T, 1979.
4. Gibbons, Ewel. *Stalking the Wild Asparagus.* New York: McKay, 1970.
5. Henderson, Zenna. "The Substitute." In *Failures.* Lexington, Mass.: Ginn and Co., 1973.
6. Lamkins, Ann. "A Model: Planning, Designing, and Evaluating Identification and Instructional Programs for Gifted, Talented, and/or Potentially Gifted Children." Albany, N.Y.: University of New York, State Education Department, 1977.
7. Macrorie, Ken. "A Room with Class." *Media and Methods* 14, no. 5 (January 1978).
8. Peacock, Tom. "Identifying American Indian Gifted and Talented." Paper presented at American Indian Gifted and Talented Planning Consortium at Bemidji, Minnesota, November 1978.
9. Pyryt, Michael. *National/State Leadership Training Institute—Gifted/Talented Newsletter*, May 1977.
10. Reid, Alistair. "Curiosity." In *Sound and Sense*, edited by Laurence Perrine. New York: Harcourt Brace Jovanovich, 1973.
10a. Renzulli, Joseph. *What Makes Giftedness: A Reexamination of the Definition of the Gifted and Talented.* Los Angeles: N/S-LTI-G/T, 1979.
11. Robinson, Halbert. "Current Myths Concerning Gifted Children." Unpublished paper, n.d.
12. Romey, Bill. *Consciousness and Creativity.* Canton, N.Y.: Ash Lad Press, 1975.
13. Solano, Cecelia. *National/State Leadership Training Institute—Gifted/Talented Newsletter*, May 1977.
14. Torrance, E.P. *Discovery and Nurturance of Giftedness in the Culturally Different.* Reston, Va.: Council for Exceptional Children, 1977.
15. Tuttle, Frederick B., Jr.; Becker, Laurence A.; and Hall, J. Beatrice. *Threat or Invitation: Teaching the Gifted.* Brockport, N.Y.: State University of New York, College at Brockport, 1977.

SUPPLEMENTARY MATERIALS

LISTS OF CHARACTERISTICS

The following lists of characteristics of gifted and talented individuals have been compiled by different educators and associations. These lists are representative of many that are available from associations for educating the gifted and talented, from educators in the field of teaching the gifted and talented, and from school systems that have developed programs for the gifted and talented. They are not necessarily the best descriptions, but they touch upon a wide variety of characteristics that are usually associated with gifted and talented individuals. While the lists provide some general indications of potential ability, the ultimate focus, however, should be on the individual student.

These lists may be used in at least two ways: (1) to describe general characteristics which can be applied to particular situations, or (2) to expand perceptions of characteristics of gifted and talented students after carefully looking at specific students in a particular school.

Characteristics of Creative-Gifted Children*

THEY—

1. Are curious
2. Have a large vocabulary
3. Have long memories
4. Sometimes learn to read alone
5. Have a keen sense of time, keep track of the date
6. Are persistent
7. Like to collect things
8. Are independent
9. Are healthy and well coordinated, but some may be delicate
10. May be bigger and stronger than average
11. Sustain interest in one or more fields over the years
12. Initiate their own activities
13. Develop earlier, sitting up, walking, talking
14. Learn easily
15. Have a keen sense of humor
16. Enjoy complicated games
17. Are creative and imaginative
18. Are interested and concerned about world problems
19. Analyze themselves, are often self-critical
20. Like older children when very young
21. Are original
22. Set high goals and ideals
23. Are leaders
24. Have talent(s) in art, music, writing, drama, dance
25. Use scientific methods of research
26. See relationships and draw sound generalizations
27. Produce work which is fresh, vital, and unique
28. Create new ideas, substances, and processes
29. Invent and build new mechanical devices
30. Often run counter to tradition
31. Continually question the status quo
32. Do the unexpected
33. Apply learning from one situation to different ones
34. Problem solve on a superior level, divergently, innovatively
35. May appear different
36. Enjoy reading, especially biography and autobiography

---

* By Ann Fabe Isaacs, National Association for Creative Children and Adults, 1976.

Some General Characteristics of Gifted Children*

The gifted child is likely to possess the following abilities:

1. To read earlier and with greater comprehension of nuances in the language.
2. To learn basic skills better. The gifted child usually learns them faster and needs less practice. Overlearning can lead to boredom, cessation of motivation, and the commission of careless errors.
3. To make abstractions when other children at the same age level cannot.
4. To delve into some interests beyond the usual limitations of childhood.
5. To comprehend, with almost nonverbal cues, implications which other children need to have "spelled out" for them.
6. To take direction independently at an earlier stage in life and to assume responsibility more naturally.
7. To maintain much longer concentration periods.
8. To express thoughts readily and to communicate with clarity in one or more areas of talent, whether verbal, numerical, aptitudinal or affective.
9. To read widely, quickly and intensely in one subject or in many areas.
10. To expend seemingly limitless energy.
11. To manifest creative and original verbal or motor responses.
12. To demonstrate a more complex processing of information than the average child of the same age.
13. To respond and relate well to peers, parents, teachers, and adults who likewise function easily in the higher-level thinking processes.
14. To have many projects going, particularly at home, so that the talented child is either busily occupied or looking for something to do.
15. To assume leadership roles because the innate sense of justice that is often noticeable in gifted children and youth gives them strength to which other young people respond.

* By Paul Plowman and others, California State Department of Education, 1971.

Behaviors in Six Talent Areas*

Convergent Thinking and Behavior

Usually responds more quickly and appropriately to questions than others his/her age.

Usually responds more quickly and appropriately than peers in new situations.

Asks questions relative to the topic or subject under discussion.

Usually selects the best course of action, the preferred outcome, or the most accurate response given several alternatives.

Sometimes re-defines a problem, a situation, or a statement made by someone else.

Sometimes determines what should be done having previously learned the appropriate procedure for achievement of a goal or task.

After considering a problem sometimes organizes activities to solve the problem.

Has on occasion given directions to others and has also written or told the procedures for performing a task.

Demonstrates through discussion, or in writing, an understanding of limitations or constraints that relate to a given problem or situation.

Has on occasion appropriately explained the reasons for making a given choice or acting a certain way.

Divergent/Creative Thinking and Behavior

Generates many ideas.

Plays with ideas and is willing to go beyond the usual or known.

Often establishes new relationships between previously unrelated objects or ideas.

Is not easily discouraged by setbacks, but will adapt and continue working on a task.

Demonstrates the ability to express ideas through many forms of communication (e.g., speaking, writing, drawing, and acting).

Understands and appreciates the humor of others and displays a sense of humor.

Often initiates learning activities (a self-starter).

Often supports an opinion or solution contrary to that selected by others (parents, teachers, peers) and ably defends his/her position.

Often values the processes of discovery and creation as much as the end product.

Relies on self-evaluation and self-support as well as evaluation and support from others.

---

* From "Talent Category Explanation Sheet" by Robert A. Male, Associate Director, GIFTS (Guidance Institute for Talented Students), University of Wisconsin-Madison, 1979.

Goal-Related Thinking and Behavior

Plans ahead by having on hand materials needed to undertake specific activities.

Has demonstrated that he/she can state what needs to be done first, second, and so on when undertaking an activity or project.

Has demonstrated the ability to define the final goal or outcome of an activity or project.

Has stated a planned course of action and acted according to the plan.

Demonstrates his/her consideration of one's abilities, time, and personal limitations when making plans.

Has identified and stated personal qualities and talents which represent strengths and limitations relative to a specific activity.

Has, when acting according to a plan, adapted it and his/her behaviors to meet changing conditions.

Has on occasion identified and stated possible contributions of others in a proposed group activity.

Has demonstrated the ability to state and define his/her own goals and priorities and to understand the goals and priorities of others even when not the same as his/her own.

Has shown that he/she can evaluate the results of following a plan by the contributions of others as well as his/her own, and the value of the plan itself.

Social Skills and Behavior

Often relates well with older children and adults.

Acknowledges the rights of others.

Values the ideas of teachers or parents.

Values the ideas of peers.

Likes to share experiences with peers.

Understands peers' humor and displays his/her own sense of humor.

Humor is understood by peers.

Ideas are respected by peers.

Demonstrates independent action which is accepted and understood by peers.

Is looked to by others for leadership.

Physical Skills and Behavior

Learns a physical skill more quickly and correctly than peers.

Is able to integrate newly learned physical skills into his/her repertoire more easily and quickly than peers.

Accurately identifies his/her physical abilities and limitations.

Physically adapts more easily than his/her peers to unanticipated circumstances or events.

Often experiments with previously learned physical skills in order to expand upon them.

Is not easily discouraged by setbacks but will adapt and continue working on physical tasks.

Accurately describes and assesses his/her own physical accomplishments and the accomplishments of others.

Has successfully taught others how to perform physical activities.

Evaluates his/her performance against an internal standard of excellence as well as established external criteria.

Demonstrates justifiable confidence in his/her physical abilities and is recognized by others as possessing superior physical abilities.

Affective Thinking and Behavior

Has shown more interest than peers in understanding self.

Has shown more of an interest than peers in understanding the attitudes and feelings of others.

Has shown more interest than peers in understanding social issues.

Communicates thoughts and feelings more easily than peers.

Recognizes and discusses more effectively than peers the similarities and differences between his/her perceptions and those of others.

Has identified certain social and interpersonal issues as important to himself/herself.

Sometimes discusses social issues with informed others.

Understands the values underlying the social issues which interest him/her.

Demonstrates a consistency in social behaviors and attitude which reflects an internalized value system.

Has modified his/her value system or philosophy based on learning.

ACTIVITIES FOR TEACHERS

The following activities have been constructed to help teachers explore the underlying issues to be considered when examining characteristics of gifted individuals. Starting with an exercise to encourage insights, the activities continue through a series of exercises to develop self-awareness, followed by a general discussion of the definition of the term "gifted," and culminate in several worksheets to assist teachers in considering students for a specific program.

1. RIPPLES

When a pebble, heavy object, or sometimes a new idea is thrown or dropped into a quiet pool, concentric waves result which reach out ever wider and wider. Sometimes such a single thought or question may summarize a theory, clarify a thought, or provide a new insight into a complex issue. The following comments are presented, not to provide answers, but to generate ripples for which we do not presume to know the boundaries.

The individual differences among the children are so great that we have become uncomfortable about any generalizations about what "gifted children" are like. (Jackson and Robinson 1977)

. . . the creative syndrome is really a set of personality characteristics distinguished by a strong self-concept that pays little attention to the academic and social sanctions that force most of us to not use all our skills for fear of social disapproval. (Gallagher, *Teaching the Gifted Child* [Allyn and Bacon], 1975)

A teacher of gifted learners may learn as much from the students as the students learn from the teacher.

It shouldn't hurt to be a kid.

The talented do what they can and the gifted do what they must. (Bill, a gifted student)

Add some of your own ripples.

2. SELF-AWARENESS

The purpose of these activities is to examine your own attitudes toward and relationship with gifted students. Be honest with yourself.

2.1 Check the characteristics in the following list* which you prefer students to exhibit in class and cross out those which you do not prefer.

_____ Adventurous	_____ Never bored
_____ Affectionate	_____ Negativistic
_____ Altruistic	_____ Obedient
_____ Always asking questions	_____ Persistent
_____ Attempts difficult jobs	_____ Popular, well liked by peers
_____ A self-starter	_____ Prefers complex tasks
_____ A good guesser	_____ Physically strong
_____ Bashful	_____ Quiet
_____ Becomes preoccupied with tasks	_____ Receptive to ideas of others
_____ Conforming	_____ Regresses occasionally (playful, childish)
_____ Considerate of others	_____ Reserved
_____ Courageous in conviction	_____ Remembers well
_____ Courteous	_____ Self-confident
_____ Competitive	_____ Self-assertive
_____ Critical of others	_____ Self-sufficient
_____ Curious	_____ Sense of humor
_____ Desires to excel	_____ Sense of beauty
_____ Determination	_____ Sincere
_____ Domineering	_____ Spirited in disagreement
_____ Disturbs procedures or organization	_____ Strives for distant goals
_____ Does work on time	_____ Stubborn
_____ Emotional	_____ Timid
_____ Emotionally sensitive	_____ Thorough
_____ Energetic	_____ Talkative
_____ Fault-finding	_____ Unsophisticated
_____ Haughty and self-satisfied	_____ Unwilling to accept things on mere say-so
_____ Healthy	_____ Versatile
_____ Independent in judgment	_____ Visionary
_____ Independent in thinking	_____ Willing to take risks
_____ Industrious	_____ Willing to accept judgments of authorities
_____ Likes to work alone	
_____ Intuitive	

---

* From _Gifted Children in the Classroom_ by E. Paul Torrance (New York: Macmillan, 1965).

2.2 Compare the characteristics you checked with other lists of characteristics of gifted and talented.

2.3 Select a student who has not performed well in your class and ask him/her about activities or interests outside of school. When you find an area of interest, ask the student to teach you more about it. This would be especially insightful if done with students from cultures different from yours.

3. YOUR SCHOOL

The purpose of this activity is to focus attention on the general attitude of teachers toward their students and to consider the implications these attitudes may have on gifted and talented individuals in the school.

3.1 Following are descriptions of five students.* Which student would be favored by most of the teachers in your school? Rank them from most desirable to least desirable according to the preferences and attitudes you believe are held by other teachers in your school.

_____ Student 1. Affectionate, considerate of others, courteous, does work on time, industrious, obedient, remembers well, willing to accept judgments of his elders, not bashful, does not disturb existing organization and procedures, not talkative.

_____ Student 2. Considerate of others, a self-starter, courteous, strong determination, independent thinker, industrious, good sense of humor, sincere, not domineering, does not disturb existing organization and procedure, not timid or bashful, curious.

_____ Student 3. Courageous in convictions, curious, independent in thinking and judgment, becomes absorbed and preoccupied with tasks, intuitive, persistent, unwilling to accept things on mere say-so, willing to take risks, not willing to accept judgments of authorities.

_____ Student 4. Socially well adjusted, conforming to behavioral norms, willing to accept judgments of authorities, obedient, courteous, prompt in doing work, neat and orderly, reserved, popular, and well liked by peers.

_____ Student 5. Adventurous, attempts difficult tasks, curious, independent in judgment and thinking, industrious, self-confident, good sense of humor, sincere, not bashful or timid, not domineering, does not disturb existing organization and procedure.

3.2 Compare the characteristics of the most and least desirable students with lists of characteristics of gifted and talented students. Are the characteristics of the gifted students valued highly in your school?

---

* From *Gifted Children in the Classroom* by E. Paul Torrance (New York: Macmillan, 1965).

4. EXPLORING DEFINITIONS OF "GIFTED"

The purpose of this group activity is to explore various concepts and opinions about the gifted and talented. The concluding "definition" should not be considered final until other factors such as program goals and characteristics have been thoroughly discussed.

4.1 Say the word "gifted," and have each person write the first word or association that comes to mind.

4.2 Say the word "gifted" again, and have each person write another word or association that comes to mind.

4.3 Repeat this as often as possible over a three-minute period.

4.4 After the participants have completed the task, have them work in small groups to compare associations and to derive an initial definition of "gifted." These definitions may then be discussed by the full group.

4.5 Compare the group definitions with those others have derived (which follow). Any definition of gifted and talented carries with it implications for selection and program development. Some may call for extensive testing and selection, while others may look toward more inclusive procedures and open situations. Some may aim toward benefiting society, while others may look toward academic achievement as an end. As you read the following definitions, consider the various philosophies and attitudes underlying each one and their implications for selection and program.

DeHaan and Havighurst, in *Educating Gifted Children*, speak of gifted children as children who are superior in some ability that can make them outstanding contributors to the welfare and quality of living in society.

Implications: _____

_____

_____

_____

Lewis Terman referred to gifted children as children having an IQ of 140 or above as measured by the Stanford-Binet Intelligence Scale.

Implications: _____

_____

_____

_____

42

Joseph Renzulli, University of Connecticut at Storrs, states:

> Giftedness consists of an interaction among three basic clusters of human traits—these clusters being above-average general abilities, high levels of task commitment, and high levels of creativity. Gifted and talented children are those possessing or capable of developing this composite set of traits and applying them to any potentially valuable area of human performance. Children who manifest or are capable of developing an interaction among the three clusters require a wide variety of educational opportunities and services that are not ordinarily provided through regular instructional programs. (Renzulli, *Phi Delta Kappan*, November 1978)

Implications: _____

_____

_____

_____

We learn through experience and experiencing, and no one teaches us anything. If the environment permits it, anyone can learn; and if the individual permits it, the environment will teach him everything it has to teach . . . . It is highly possible that what is called talented behavior is simply a greater individual capacity for experiencing. (Viola Spolin, in *Reach, Touch, and Teach* by Terry Borton [McGraw-Hill, 1970])

Implications: _____

_____

_____

_____

5. IMPLEMENTATION

Before surveying the potential methods and procedures for identifying gifted and talented individuals, you should have a general idea of the characteristics of the population to be selected. These characteristics, however, should be related directly to the goals of the program you plan to develop. All the characteristics of gifted individuals may not be appropriate for your goals. Indeed, some may actually interfere with student success. Gifted individuals should not be forced into programs that are inappropriate for their needs. In such cases, other programs may need to be developed. The following activities are designed to help prioritize both goals and characteristics which you feel are important for success in your program.

Prioritizing Goals: On the following lines list those goals which you believe are most appropriate for your program (e.g., develop skills in analysis, synthesis, and evaluation). Do not worry about ordering them.

A _____

B _____

C _____

D _____

E _____

F _____

G _____

H _____

I _____

Now place the letters of each goal on an appropriate line in the following "pyramid."

		_____		
	_____	_____	_____	
_____	_____	_____	_____	_____
Greatest Need	Greater Need	Mid-Need	Smaller Need	Smallest Need

Followup: Share sorting with other members of the group. Discuss reasons for placement but do not force unanimous agreement. In the following "pyramid," place letters of goals to reflect general group feelings.

		_____		
	_____	_____	_____	
_____	_____	_____	_____	_____
Greatest Need	Greater Need	Mid-Need	Smaller Need	Smallest Need

Prioritizing Characteristics: On the following lines list those characteristics which you feel are most appropriate for gifted students in your program (e.g., the student is able to see relationships among diverse ideas). Do not worry about ordering them.

A _____

B _____

C _____

D _____

E _____

F _____

G _____

H _____

I _____

J _____

K _____

L _____

M _____

N _____

O _____

P _____

Now place the letters of each characteristic on an appropriate line in the following "pyramid."

Greatest Importance	Greater Importance	Mid-Importance	Smaller Importance	Smallest Importance

Followup: Share sorting with other members of the group. Discuss reasons for placement, but do not force unanimous agreement. In the following "pyramid," place letters of characteristics to reflect general group feelings.

Greatest Importance	Greater Importance	Mid-Importance	Smaller Importance	Smallest Importance

IDENTIFICATION

How do you know what someone is really like? If the person comes to trust you, to believe you can be of help, he/she may choose to share his/her real interests, feelings, beliefs, and knowledge with you. If the person fears that you do not have his/her best interests at heart, he/she may withdraw or even come to display opposite characteristics as a way of self-protection. Our constant search for "more objective measures," which seems to be based upon the assumption that we can, in fact, obtain precise and analytical measurements of creativity, may very well be moving in the opposite direction from establishing a relationship of trust.

In *Creative Life*, Clark E. Moustakas, a professor at the Merrill-Palmer Institute of Human Development and Family Life, observes, "Three methods or attitudes of modern living contribute to the deterioration of uniqueness and individuality and the development of mass behavior and mass identity: *analysis, diagnosis,* and *evaluation.*" (10:107) He continues, "A science that objectifies, evaluates, and puts people in categories eliminates the real persons. It sets up impersonal and unalterable standards and categories based on fragmented views of behavior." (10:109) As we approach the process of choosing identification procedures, it would be well to keep in mind that the further removed we are from the person, the greater the danger that what we identify may bear a closer resemblance to the mounted insect than to the living butterfly.

Before the 1950s most educators and school systems tended to follow Louis Terman's example and based most decisions about gifted individuals on IQ and scholastic achievement scores. Standardized group intelligence tests, such as the California Tests of Mental Maturity, were often used to determine IQ. In these tests educators were looking for exceptional ability in verbal or performance IQ or a combination of the two. (7) For final identification individual IQ tests such as the Wechsler scales (WISC) and the Stanford Binet were used. Most considered an IQ of 130 or above to fall in the gifted range.

With the greater emphasis on intellectual superiority at the end of the fifties and early sixties, some educators and researchers turned their attention away from IQ and achievement scores to other areas of giftedness. J. P. Guilford, with his analysis of the human intellect and resultant Structure of the Intellect model, provided a theoretical basis for examining other facets of the individual apart from IQ. (4a) This work was highly significant as it provided both the framework and the impetus for more research into areas of intelligence other than those measured by the IQ tests. Other researchers such as Getzels and Jackson, E. Paul Torrance, Joe Khatena, and Wallach and Kogan helped create and evaluate creativity tests and methods of bringing out creativity in students. As reported by Khatena (8), E. Paul Torrance has derived several areas of creative thinking ability among which are fluency—the ability to produce many ideas; flexibility—the ability to produce different kinds of ideas; originality—the ability to produce unusual ideas; elaboration—the ability to add details to an idea; synthesis—the ability to combine two or more figures into a related whole; and closure—the ability to delay completion of a task to allow for the mental leaps that make possible the creation of original ideas.

Furthermore, the humanistic feelings of the sixties prompted many to look for more equitable ways to identify gifted individuals from different cultures and those with language difficulties. These attempts resulted in the creation of instruments that do not assume that all share common cultural and language backgrounds. Researchers at this time also attempted to identify the gifted and talented through the use of biographical inventories, behavioral checklists and ratings, and parent nominations.

Although researchers have long considered these other identification procedures to be important, until recently most school systems have relied primarily on standardized tests and teacher nominations. With the rapid growth of interest in services for the mentally and physically handicapped during the sixties and early seventies, many schools shelved all identification procedures for the gifted. In 1972 the U.S. Office of Education Report showed a renewed federal interest in the gifted which began to have its effect on schools throughout the country. (2) This time many schools attempted to examine several areas of giftedness. Consequently, educators have begun to look for a variety of identification instruments that can help them locate a wide range of gifted and talented individuals.

When considering various procedures for selecting students for a program, the decision should be made as to whether the approach will be "exclusive" or "inclusive." With an "exclusive" stand, screening efforts are focused on ensuring that no students without gifted ability will be admitted to the program. The admission requirements will be exceptionally stringent, accepting only a small percentage quota, such as the top two percent. This means, however, that although the students in the program will probably be of superior ability, many other students who are equally gifted but who, for several reasons, did not perform well on the screening instruments will be overlooked. When an "inclusive" attitude toward screening is adopted, a wide variety of instruments and procedures with more flexible admission scores is selected. While this approach provides for the selection of names of the gifted students, some students who may not actually possess superior ability but who perform well on the screening instruments will also be admitted.

A program in rural Maine uses six ways of nominating gifted and talented students: parent nomination, questionnaires, teacher nomination, and self-nomination, the top ten percent of group IQ test, and the top ten percent of grades. Students identified by three of the six methods are automatically included, and those identified by one or two are considered on a case study basis. A conscious decision to be inclusive was made at the start of the program.

The decision to be exclusive or inclusive should be a conscious one because, ultimately, it will affect the program and curriculum. The exclusive attitude enables the teacher to construct activities aimed solely at students with superior abilities. A program of rapid acceleration exemplifies this approach. The inclusive attitude, however, calls for a more flexible curriculum with provision for students to enter and leave without penalty.

Before beginning a program for gifted students, the program developers have to define a population which will benefit from the program. The selection of the population involves identifying those students who possess the specific characteristics necessary for success in the particular program for the gifted envisioned for the particular school within the community. If all programs, communities, resources, and students were the same, the identification process would be routine. Each program, however, is different since all the other factors affecting the program goals—community, teachers, and resources—are unique.

Consequently, the identification process involves much more than merely selecting those students who score highest on a standardized test or who have the highest grades.

In general, the criteria for identification should not be specified until the goals of the program have been defined and the general program format has been established. Once these elements have been clarified, a screening committee can begin to examine various devices for identifying gifted characteristics in light of the goals and format of the particular program. In some instances, however, the school may discover a gifted student through a variety of methods and then design a program specifically to allow that student to develop his or her gifts. This approach is similar to the Individualized Educational Program (IEP) required for the handicapped under Public Law 94–142. While the methods and procedures to be described are aimed at the former type of program development, the school should always be open to the individualized approach where programs are developed for specific individuals and their unique characteristics.

Although some general tests of mental ability are already being used in many school districts, the screening committee should initially examine many different methods equally. The committee should (1) determine which devices measure the specific characteristics required by the program; (2) decide which of these methods would be the most feasible for the district in terms of facilities, budget, and personnel; and (3) establish an identification procedure, outlining the various steps to take to locate those students for whom the particular program is designed. (See also Ruth Martinson, *The Identification of the Gifted and Talented* (9).)

TYPES OF IDENTIFICATION INSTRUMENTS AND PROCEDURES

The discussion which follows describes various methods of screening and some of their limitations and advantages which should be taken into account.

Standardized Group Tests

Many systems use standardized group tests of IQ and achievement to select students for a gifted program because of their seeming objectivity and ease of administration. Such tests do, however, contain some limitations which may invalidate their use as sole indicators of superior ability. First, as group tests they have been designed for the average student. Consequently, most of the questions are far below the challenging level of the superior student; the ceilings are too low to discriminate between the bright student and the gifted student. In addition, the questions are usually aimed at lower cognitive levels such as recall and comprehension rather than at the higher ones, such as synthesis and evaluation, which are more appropriate for the gifted.

> Any instruments chosen for testing should include enough difficult items to allow for differentiation among children who are performing at the upper end of the scale. Bright children may perform like average children unless they are presented with sufficiently challenging material. (5)

Second, these tests achieve their "objectivity" by limiting responses to selection of "correct" answers chosen from various alternatives. One of the characteristics of many gifted individuals is the ability to see beyond the obvious answer and recognize situations in which a seemingly "wrong" answer may indeed be "correct." These students are often confused by the limited areas of responses granted by the group tests.

When Joseph took the IQ test, he was puzzled by several questions since many of the answers seemed correct to him and he could select only one per question. One question, for example, showed a man playing basketball and asked if this were work or play. While many students could easily respond "play," Joseph had difficulty as he realized that for a professional basketball player this was "work" rather than play.

Third, most of these tests, especially after third grade, rely heavily on the printed word and standard English. Students who have reading problems or who do not share the same cultural backgrounds as those for whom the test was designed may not perform well. Many gifted students are overlooked because they fall into either or both of these groups.

In an extensive investigation of the comparable effectiveness of several methods of identifying gifted students, Pegnato and Birch found that group IQ tests failed to identify nearly fifty percent of the students who scored above 125 on an individual IQ test. (11) If the identification committee had used a score of 125 or better on a group IQ test as a basis for selecting students for a program, the committee would have missed approximately half of the students who achieved that score or better on an individualized IQ test. While many gifted students would have been included in the program, nearly half of the gifted students in the school would have been excluded.

A dramatic example is provided by Keith. As a six-year-old first grade student, he scored 98 on a group IQ test, 170 on an individual test, and at ceiling on a math reasoning test.

A revealing account of the power of IQ scores in the minds of people in spite of a specific attempt to discount their validity may be found in "Teachers Don't Want to Be Labeled" by Harry W. Forgon. (3)

Culture Fair Tests

Many have criticized standardized tests for being culturally biased. Most such tests assume a common cultural background in terms of associations, experiences, and verbal facility with the English language as spoken by the majority of students in the United States. While any test will probably contain items with particular cultural associations or biases, many have found that individuals from minority groups with cultural backgrounds different from the majority fare better on nonverbal tests. (14) Consequently, some schools with large minority populations have used culture fair tests which rely heavily on nonverbal items rather than on verbal questions and responses. The Columbia Tests of Mental Maturity, for example, require the individual to select appropriate responses from several figural items. The individual's response is nonverbal, as are the items in the questions. Torrance has found (15) that many creativity tests because of their nonverbal nature are also indicators of gifted ability in individuals from minority groups.

Creativity Tests

If a school is planning a program to promote creativity in gifted individuals, the tests mentioned previously may perhaps be inappropriate since they fail to indicate traits commonly associated with creativity. Indeed, these tests often penalize such traits by requiring a single, correct answer. Currently the most widely used instruments for identifying creatively gifted individuals are the Torrance Tests of Creative Thinking (1974). Looking for fluency, flexibility, originality, and elaboration skills, the items consist mostly of open-ended questions or task completion exercises. Although some studies have found high correlations between the Torrance Tests and IQ tests (Torrance 1966), with gifted individuals the correlations have been low (Dellas and Gaier 1976), indicating that the Torrance tests may measure areas different from those measured by IQ tests. (1) Several other tests have also been developed to measure aspects of creativity, many of which are cited by Carolyn Callahan. (1)

In addition to tests, however, developers may also look at examples of student creativity. This may be accomplished by having individuals perform creative tasks within their immediate environments, either school or neighborhood, or by examining student products. This personal approach may be more appropriate for students in cultures different from the majority and for programs which focus on particular kinds of creativity, such as creative writing. When evaluating these creative products, developers should be sure that the evaluator has both expertise in the specific area of creativity and familiarity with the culture which the individual represents.

Individual IQ Tests

Although they focus on general intellectual ability, only one of several areas of giftedness, individual IQ tests, such as the Stanford-Binet or the WISC-R, are usually the final screening instrument in most schools. Implicit in the use of the individual IQ test as the *final* screening instrument is the assumption that it does, in fact, identify with precision and accuracy who is and who is not "gifted." Since such tests are administered individually, the examiner can note quality of responses as well as correctness. In addition, the interview atmosphere of the testing situation also allows the examiner to make the individual more comfortable and less threatened by the testing situation.

Individual IQ tests, however, and even creativity tests, like the group tests are only reflections of what the individual is capable of producing. All represent an attempt to quantify through paper and pencil efforts the potential quality of a student's ability. In order to determine an individual's ability or potential, a broader perspective should be obtained, one which views the actual works the student produces in specific areas. Some of the following procedures may allow this perspective.

52

Behavior Rating Scales

In an effort to focus attention directly on the individual student, some educators have constructed behavior rating scales or checklists of behaviors indicative of gifted ability in specific areas. Instruments such as the "Scales for Rating the Behavioral Characteristics of Superior Students," sample items from which appear in Supplementary Materials, list specific characteristics and illustrative behaviors of gifted individuals. (13a) The task of an observer using rating scales is to check presence or absence of a particular behavior in an individual, rate the strength of the behavior, or list individuals from a group who possess the particular characteristics under consideration. While these scales do allow the observer to view the individual directly without the intermediary of a test, they also present several difficulties. (See Supplementary Materials.)

The first difficulty when using the scales is that many observers have different interpretations of the various characteristics and place different emphases on behaviors indicative of the particular characteristic. The question of emphasis causes problems with interpreting presence or absence of a characteristic and even more with interpreting strength of a characteristic.

After using a well-known rating scale for identifying gifted individuals for a particular program, the teachers found that not only had they interpreted the ratings differently, but they had even interpreted the indicative behaviors differently. They could not, for example, agree on the difference between a ranking of 2 or 4 on "persistent in reaching a goal."

A second difficulty lies in the time individual ratings require of teachers. If asked to rate each of one hundred thirty students on each of seventy-five characteristics, the teacher may resent the time and effort required to accomplish the task. This resentment may cause problems with both the rankings of the ratings of individual students and with future support of the program. One way to alleviate this potential source of difficulty would be to involve all teachers in a discussion of the identification, especially ratings of characteristics, before they are asked to perform the task. Another way to reduce the burden would be to have teachers discuss the most important characteristics and indicative behaviors and then list only those students who demonstrate those particular characteristics most frequently.

Teacher Nomination

Perhaps the most prevalent method of identifying gifted individuals is to ask for teacher recommendations. This method, however, has been shown in research studies to be ineffective. In their study, Pegnato and Birch found that junior high school teachers not only failed to nominate over fifty percent of the gifted individuals in the school (11), but they also identified many average students as gifted. Jacobs's investigation of the ability of primary teachers to correctly identify gifted students in their classes was even more dismaying. He found that they were able to identify only ten percent of the gifted individuals who were indicated through the use of an individual IQ test. (6)

The failure of teachers to identify gifted individuals accurately may reflect their inability to recognize behaviors indicative of giftedness. Usually teachers tend to emphasize such behaviors as neatness, punctuality, answering correctly, and cooperation which are not necessarily traits of gifted individuals. As discussed previously, gifted individuals often possess characteristics which are in opposition to these behaviors. The divergent or associative thinker, for example, may make leaps in logic and provide an answer far beyond the particular response sought by the teacher; but, because of considerations of time and the interest of most of the other students, the teacher may be unable to pursue such an answer and may therefore regard it as incorrect. The gifted student may thus receive poor recommendations and average or even poor grades.

Teacher nomination, however, need not be inadequate. When provided with guidelines and in-service work on the characteristics and behaviors of gifted individuals, teachers become much more accurate in their perceptions. (4) In-service training in the characteristics of gifted individuals is valuable not only for the identification of students for a gifted program, but also as an aid for the individual classroom teacher. An increased sensitivity to the characteristics and behaviors of gifted individuals enables the teacher to become more aware of the potential of all students.

Transcripts

Along with teacher nomination, the student's scholastic record is often used to aid in the identification process. Grades can be as misleading as they are helpful, however. As mentioned previously, when evaluation occurs the relationship between the person making the evaluation and the person being evaluated is often crucial. Most transcripts have no way of elaborating upon relationships; they merely present a symbol which is intended to represent certain levels of competency. In addition, grades often reflect perceptions of appropriate classroom behavior rather than actual ability. In the case of the highly gifted student who is frustrated and bored, several poor or failing grades on a transcript might not be surprising to an evaluator who is familiar with negative behaviors of some gifted students.

Biographical Inventories

As part of an identification procedure, information should be gathered about the individual's interests and background outside school as well as performance within the classroom. Often gifted individuals display more of the superior abilities in extracurricular activities than they do in the classroom. Biographical and interest inventories can provide insights into these individuals which might otherwise be overlooked. Such inventories may be in the form of multiple-choice items, checklists, open-ended questions, or any combination. Since a general inventory can be valuable for all teachers, the screening committee might highlight those behaviors and interests which are felt to indicate success in the particular program. "Scores" can be derived from the inventory on the basis of appropriate responses to questions concerning behaviors and interests pertinent to the program envisioned. The Institute for Behavioral Research in Creativity in Salt Lake City found its own biographical inventory (see Supplementary Materials) was very effective in predicting students with high potential for academic talent, leadership ability, and artistic or musical talent. (16) In some parts of the country parents may consider certain questions on biographical inventories invasions of privacy. Consequently, the items should be carefully considered for appropriateness and value to the identification process. This situation will vary according to the local conditions and program.

Parent Recommendation

In addition to his consideration of primary teachers, Jacobs also evaluated the effectiveness of parents in identifying gifted children. He found that parents were able to select sixty-one percent of the gifted children and, in addition, showed less tendency than teachers to overestimate abilities. (6) This finding is not surprising when we consider that parents observe children more frequently than teachers and in more relaxed, informal situations. Often gifted individuals display their true abilities under these circumstances, while in the classroom they may tend either to conform to the rest of the class or to fall into the category of "misfit."

Obtaining information from parents sometimes presents a problem for program developers because they do not wish to give the impression that all the children will be admitted to a particular program; nor do they want to incur the frustration and wrath of those parents whose children are not selected. One way to secure the necessary information without indicating admission to a program is to gather it as part of the routine for all instruction. This can be as a checklist of activities and interests or as a multiple-choice biographical inventory. Jackson and Robinson found that while checklists and multiple choices provided valuable information, supplementary anecdotes gave necessary insights into the quality of the behaviors demonstrated by the children. (5) For example, although several parents might indicate that their children read at an early age, a description of what was read, how it was read, and when it was read would be even more revealing. There is a difference between reading a picture book and reading the *Winnie the Pooh* series by age five. Such information would be valuable to all teachers and, at the same time, could be used to help select gifted individuals.

Peer Recommendation

Although not given enough importance by many, student evaluations can provide valuable insights into the abilities of their peers. Usually, the teacher's perception of student ability is limited to contact within the classroom and as an adult to a child. Student contact with classmates may allow for more demonstration of some of the characteristics previously discussed than may be shown in the classroom setting. Leadership ability, for example, may take a different form outside class from inside. Even general intellectual abilities may become more evident to classmates than to teachers since many gifted individuals are wary of demonstrating their abilities in the school setting.

In an effort to gather information about peer recommendations, one school presented each student with a list of questions such as "Whom would you ask for help on a composition?" Students were then asked to list three individuals in the class, as it was believed that they might feel obligated to list their best friends first, regardless of ability. In reviewing the lists, the committee looked for repetition of names rather than just names of students who were listed first by peers.

RECOMMENDED PROCEDURES

Many researchers are finding that a combination of approaches appears to be the most effective method of identifying gifted and talented students. Renzulli and Smith compared a traditional approach comprised of group ability tests and individual IQ tests with a case study approach comprised of aptitude and/or achievement scores, ratings by past and/or present teachers, past performance, parent ratings, and self-ratings. (13) They found the case study method is generally superior to the traditional approach in identifying gifted students, especially among minority groups. In addition, they found this approach less costly and less time-consuming than the traditional method. While many would concur that the case study approach is more effective, they would be surprised at the finding that it is also more efficient.

Jackson and Robinson (5) provide additional guidance for identifying the gifted and talented, especially at the preschool level. First, they suggest that children be allowed several opportunities to demonstrate their intellectual and creative skills. Second, instead of taking an individual's average score across various instruments, as is often done, the identification committee should consider the child's best performance and include him or her in the program on that basis. Third, Jackson and Robinson found that parents' anecdotes of their children's behaviors may give more insight into early giftedness than testing situations or questionnaires and checklists. Finally, the researchers strongly suggest that any identification procedure be "tied to the program for which the children are being identified."

Pfleger, in his extensive report on the research and guidance laboratory at the University of Wisconsin, presents several premises for identification. He suggests that the identification procedure should contain a variety of techniques and should continue over a long time. He recommends that at least some of the identification techniques should be individualized, taking into account the cultural-experiential environment of the individual. Pfleger also suggests that the process requires systematic involvement of professionals who observe the individual directly and understand her/his cultural background. To examine individual performance, both self-chosen and required efforts should be assessed. (12)

The identification procedure may be viewed as a two-stage process. The first stage consists of screening individuals through group tests, teacher nominations (by teachers trained in recognizing gifted individuals), peer recommendations, and other generally pertinent information geared to the specific kind of gifted program envisioned.

In the second stage, based on a student's best effort rather than an average of scores, the screening committee selects a smaller number of students for more individualized identification. Special consideration should be given those students on the fringe—those with culturally different backgrounds, language difficulties, and records of discontent. In the second screening stage individuals should be given several opportunities to demonstrate exceptional ability in the specific areas to be developed in the program. These opportunities may include biographical inventory, interviews, parental anecdotes, and examination of such student work as papers, paintings, films, or dramatizations.

When making final decisions for the program, the committee should try to include all students who might excel in it. Several considerations may help with this determination. First, admission into the program should be based on an indication of potential and "best" performances, not on an average of test scores or accomplishment. When teachers are asked to recommend students, they should be sure to discuss the indicative behaviors and the goals of the program. The instruments selected should have sufficiently high ceilings to allow gifted students room to excel. Many standardized tests, especially for lower grade levels, do not provide for these superior abilities. The final selection should be based on information gathered from a variety of sources which examine the characteristics pertinent to the specific program.

In addition to these program concerns, there are also several political considerations which may affect the program. Early in the process, a decision should be made regarding pressure from influential parents whose children do not belong in the program. Strong administrative support either way will be required as the teacher will not have the authority to stand alone. Also, the individual's right to privacy should always be respected. No questions should violate this right even indirectly. Questions concerning income, social status, and religion do not provide vital information for identification but do intrude.

The following material from the New York State Education Department provides nineteen detailed steps for establishing and implementing a general identification procedure. (10a)

Implementing An Identification Program

Task	Activity	Product	Resource
PHASE ONE: PLANNING			
1. Identify leadership	as determined by local district	one assigned person who has support of the superintendent and board of education, and others from the school and community to serve as a task group	
	develop and understanding of gifted/talented students and programs in general		
2. Conduct a needs assessment	survey student characteristics	assessment of local test scores and profiles of students' capabilities and achievements as indicated by intelligence and achievement test scores	subjective and objective information from teachers, counselors, psychologists, and administrators
	survey student interests	results of an interest survey	STUDENT INTEREST SURVEY
	survey curricular and extracurricular provisions/programs currently available within the school	assessment of local district provisions/programs for gifted/talented and degree of teacher interest and commitment	teachers and administrators
	survey community interests and provisions for programs	assessment of community interest and possibilities for support of specific programs	parents, members of the community and civic organizations and clubs
		recommendation to maintain current provisions/programs, strengthen existing ones, or develop new options	New York State Education Department publication **A Survey of Education for the Gifted and Talented in New York State in 1974–75**

Task	Activity	Product	Resource
PHASE TWO: ORGANIZING			
3. Develop statement of philosophy for meeting the needs and interests of the gifted and talented	involve parents, educators, and members of the community	statement of philosophy accepted by local board of education	New York State Education Department Position Paper No. 23, **Educating the Gifted and Talented in New York State**
	relate local district philosophy to the special needs of the gifted in a written document to be approved by the board of education		
4. Provide awareness among faculty	present awareness workshop(s) which bring teachers up to date on data from needs assessment activities and findings	faculty motivated to go into PHASE THREE	Board of Cooperative Educational Services, Local, and State Education Department personnel
5. Develop a written plan for activities in PHASES THREE and FOUR	analyze this model and adapt it to local needs; include personnel designations, time lines, and objectives	written plan, approved by administration	teachers, administrators, parents, and members of the community
PHASE THREE: SET PRIORITIES			
6. Identify one or more **specific** fields for K–12 programming; i.e., biological sciences rather than "science," gymnastics rather than "movement"	identify societal and community concerns and resources	list of human and technical resources categorized by area (music, art, science, et al.)	
	analyze results of student interest survey	summary of students' specific interests (types, locations, age levels, continuity)	results of previously administered STUDENT INTEREST SURVEY
Identify a target group (gifted, talented, potentially gifted) for identification and programming	match student needs, characteristics, and interests with current district and community opportunities		teachers, administrators, parents, members of community, and yellow pages of telephone books

Task	Activity	Product	Resource
	identify gaps where interested students have no opportunities identify teacher strengths identify program strengths list programs, facilities, events, and people in the community who do or could provide systematic instructional opportunities for gifted/talented students	recommendations for program priorities	suggested criteria: • high student interest • competent instruction available • materials and facilities available
7. Inform teachers and parents; gain their interest, support, and commitment	use faculty meetings, conference days, newsletters, et al., for inservice and communication	increased cooperation	
8. Allocate resources	persuade the Board of Education to allocate or reallocate resources to meet the needs of talented and gifted students	a budget	administrators, parents, members of the community, and advocacy groups

PHASE FOUR: NOMINATION AND IDENTIFICATION

Task	Activity	Product	Resource
9. Determine broad program goals, objectives, and evaluation plan	study the literature; analyze existing programs in other school districts	written program goals, objectives, and general evaluation plan for students who are functionally or potentially talented and/or gifted in fundamental skills, creative problem-finding/solving skills, and personal characteristics	the model proposed in this publication; Title IV-C projects in New York State
	provide for the collection of data: rating scales time needed for administration; inservice; evaluation; cost for revisions; objective instruments		

61

Task	Activity	Product	Resource
	cost; availability; effectiveness; provide for inservice content; amount; quality; effectiveness; costs		
10. Set program parameters	define "gifted" for local district planning purposes define "talented" and "potentially gifted" for local district planning purposes accept, adapt, or reject the model provided in this publication determine: maximum/minimum number of students to be programmed, nature of program (for talented and/or gifted); location, amount of time, resource teachers, grade levels, role of the school, role of the community	a model for identification and programming a broad description of the program, including definitions of students involved (specific objectives for curriculum and instruction will need to be written in terms of the needs and characteristics of identified students)	this publication, professional journals, and consultants
11. Set criteria for selection of students	study the literature; analyze this publication	criteria for final selection (number, age levels, et al.)	
12. Develop nomination instruments	as an inservice activity involve teachers in the process of adapting the nomination forms provided in this guide identify a task group to manage nomination process	locally designed nomination forms	suggested criteria: information requested should (1) be program specific; (2) provide for a broad sweep of possible talented and/or gifted students; (3) be general and related primarily to performance or potential

Task	Activity	Product	Resource
			performance in activities requiring use of the fundamental and creative problem-finding/solving skills, rather than personal characteristics; (4) be independent of reading and writing
	select individuals and student groups who will be asked to make nominations		suggestions for use of nomination forms:
			the STUDENT SELF-ASSESSMENT FORM should be filled out by every student who indicated high interest in the priority area and spends a great amount of time at the activity;
			the ADULT NOMINATION FORM is intended for appropriate members of the community, educators, and parents;
			the PEER NOMINATION FORM is for all students at the grade level(s) selected for programming
13. Obtain a pool of students	make a master list of all nominated students; assign a number to each one; analyze information from SELF-ASSESSMENT FORMS	pool of students for Step 14	criteria for inclusion in pool: nomination from two sources; student indicates extensive interest and capability
14. Select instruments for collection of objective data concerning nominated students	analyze locally available objective data-gathering instruments such as group intelligence tests, individual intelligence tests,	selected instruments	criteria for selection includes: applicability to the identification model;

Task	Activity	Product	Resource
	appropriate sections of achievement tests, and standardized aptitude, personality, or creativity tests consult the literature for descriptions of additional tests		relevance and useful-ness of group IQ scores to the priority field availability of indi-vidual IQ test scores; availability of special aptitude or skill tests; availability and use-fulness of achieve-ment test scores; availability of item analysis of items of test sections related to the priority field
15. Develop/select subjective data-gathering instruments	collect rating scales from varied sources adapt rating scales to the priority area select additional subjective materials for inclusion in the selection process, such as autobiographies, cumulative records, records of counsel-ors, and parental interviews and questionnaries	rating scales for local district priority area(s) additional subjective materials	criteria includes: applicability to the identification model; appropriateness of rating scale items for fundamental skills to the priority field; appropriateness of rating scale items for creative problem-finding/solving steps and student charac-teristics; availability of oppor-tunities to rate the problem-finding/solving skills; availability of stu-dent products; availability of adults to use scales and rate student prod-ucts, processes and/or performances RATING SCALE: Fundamental Skills and Abilities

Task	Activity	Product	Resource
			RATING SCALE: Creative Problem-Finding/Solving Skills RATING SCALE: Personal Characteristics
16. Design a format for data analysis	analyze characteristics of data-gathering instruments develop summary matrices for objective and subjective data or adapt SAMPLE MATRICES included in this publication	Matrix for subjective data Matrix for objective data	criteria for summary matrices: 1) manageable format 2) easily analyzed 3) ratings must be transformed to numbers see sample summary matrices for objective and subjective data
17. Provide inservice training for use of data-collection instruments	involve teachers in the adaptation of instruments use faculty meetings to bring all faculty up to date on the processes		
18. Identify students	administer subjective and objective data gathering instruments; identify members of a Selection Committee develop criteria and cutoff points; rank students; use a cutoff figure of twice the number of stu-	Selection Committee including an administrator, a teacher, a special teacher, a guidance counselor or psychologist, a parent, and appropriate others to examine the data collected for the students group of students who meet specific selection criteria	each rating scale should be used by a minimum of two adults use products developed in Step 11

Task	Activity	Product	Resource
	dents to be accommodated by the program select decision-making committee	final selection of students for programming	
19. Evaluate identification processes and (revised) instruments	evaluate information collected	recommendations for: revised identification program; revised curriculum and instruction to facilitate identification; initiation of "threshold" programs specially designed to encourage development of talents and gifted among minorities and women	criteria may include: number of females identified compared with percentage to be expected number of functionally talented and/or gifted identified number of potentially talented and/or gifted identified number of minority students compared with expectations criteria used in Steps 14 and 15 should also be applied

Not all screening instruments and methods are appropriate for every area of gifted and talented ability. Once a general procedure for selecting gifted students for a particular program has been determined, a committee may wish to focus on instruments and methods for locating students with superior abilities in specific areas. This is a vital step in the procedure since it should ensure that the identification methods chosen do help locate students with characteristics appropriate for the particular program.

The following are some of the methods which seem to be most appropriate for identifying gifted and talented students in the respective areas defined by the U.S. Office of Education in 1978.

Intellectual Ability

GOAL: To help students expand their intellectual abilities and interests, and their modes of responding to their environment.

Students who would probably excel in these programs often display some of the following characteristics: verbal sense of humor, divergent and associative thinking, ability to generalize, questioning attitude, and persistence. To help locate these individuals, the following instruments and procedures would be helpful:

- *Student Interest Inventory.* Look for a wide variety of interests, some of which have been pursued in depth. Look for students who show a highly developed, verbal sense of humor. Also look at the games they enjoy playing, such as chess and Mastermind.
- *Parent Nomination.* Look for items similar to those cited under interest inventory. Also look for hobbies, books read, and games.
- *Peer Nomination.* Look for students who are sought out for answers to both academic and general problems.
- *Teacher Recommendation.* Look for students who ask a variety of questions, who tend to ask probing questions, who have strong interests, who are critical of superficial answers.

- *Biographical Inventory.* Highlight those activities and interests which demonstrate variety and some depth and persistence. Also look for behaviors which reflect a curiosity about the total environment.
- *Objective Tests.* While we have many reservations about the use of standardized tests, especially group tests (see pp. 49–51), some gifted and talented individuals demonstrate their abilities on individual intelligence tests. These tests, however, should be used to include individuals rather than to exclude them. If students do not perform well on these tests, they may still be gifted and may show it in some of the ways just mentioned.
- *Tests of Higher-Level Thinking Skills.* See "Sources of Instruments" in Supplementary Materials.
- If there is a large group of individuals whose cultural backgrounds differ from the majority, *culture fair* or some *creativity tests* may be used.

Academic Talent

GOAL: To help students pursue academic interests in depth.

Students with superior academic talent usually achieve well in the academic areas, have superior reading and verbal abilities. They may be identified by using the following instruments and procedures:

- *Interest Inventory.* Look for strong interests in the academic area(s) included in the program.
- *Parent Recommendation.* Look for activities and interests which reflect ability, depth of knowledge, and interest in the subjects included in the program.
- *Transcripts.* Look for high grades in specific areas.
- *Teacher Recommendation.* Ask for recommendations especially from teachers of subject areas or disciplines related to the program.
- *Tests.* Achievement tests, especially in subject(s) in the program; intelligence tests; and special tests for specific subject(s) in the program may be used.

Creative and Productive Thinking

> GOAL: To provide a wide range of opportunities and experiences to allow individuals to experiment, take risks, and produce creative *products*.

Students with superior creative and productive thinking abilities enjoy exploring "What if . . ." questions, generating a wide variety of possible answers to real and hypothetical situations, and drawing relationships among seemingly unrelated ideas. These individuals are often absorbed in the literature of science fiction. They may be identified by use of the following instruments and procedures:

- *Self-Interest Inventory*. Look for a variety of diverse interests and activities and for enjoyment in creating products and pursuing ideas.
- *Parent Recommendation*. Look for diversity of interests, sense of humor, involvement in futures studies (e.g., science fiction, environmental progress, scientific advances).
- *Teacher Recommendation*. Focus on behaviors demonstrating abilities to draw associations among seemingly diverse ideas and abilities to generate many ideas from a specific stimulus. Also look for students who often raise "What if . . ." questions and who show an interest in implications of current trends for the future.
- *Biographical Inventory*. Highlight diversity of interests, variety of modes of expression other than print (e.g., film, tapes, verbal).
- *Student Products*. Look for both originality and quality.
- *Tests*. See Supplementary Materials, "Creativity Tests."

Leadership

> GOAL: To help students fulfill their potential as leaders in our society.

Students with superior leadership ability are often those whom others respect and follow. These are also the individuals who are willing to assume responsibility for a variety of tasks and to fulfill this responsibility once accepted. The following instruments and procedures are suggested to identify them:

- *Self-Interest Inventory.* Focus on those areas which demonstrate a willingness to assume responsibility and a desire to complete tasks.
- *Biographical Inventory.* Take special note of activities which reflect group experiences, project work.
- *Peer Recommendation.* Look for those students others would like to assume responsibility for group tasks and those who others believe will complete the task well. Also look for students whom others select to participate in their groups.
- *Teacher Recommendation.* Focus on students to whom other students turn for help in completing projects, including nonacademic areas. These students may not be the ones teachers would necessarily select for the tasks. Also consider students who contribute productively to group efforts even when they are not leading the group.
- *Sociometric Tests.* Look for students who have influence over others in informal situations.

Visual and Performing Arts

GOAL: To provide opportunities and experiences to allow gifted and talented students to develop their abilities in specific areas in the visual and/or performing arts (e.g., painting, sculpture, film, dance, theatre, music).

Students with superior abilities in the visual and performing arts often pursue these interests through extracurricular school activities, community functions, and, especially, individually. Consequently, behaviors indicative of these gifted individuals may be found beyond the classroom. The following instruments and procedures are recommended to identify them:

- *Self-Interest Inventory.* Look for pursuit of interests in visual or performing arts. These activities or hobbies may include photography, folk art, painting, drawing, music, and dance.

70

- *Parent Recommendation.* Look for early interests and activities in visual and performing arts, including both attendance and participation.
- *Biographical Inventory.* Highlight activities and interests in the preceding areas.
- *Product.* Have experts in specific visual and performing arts areas examine an individual work or performance, looking both for quality and potential.
- *Personal Interview.* Because of the intensive nature of some of the work in this area, look for students who are willing to expend the necessary time and energy. Furthermore, some students are not aware of the variety of opportunities within this field, therefore the interview situation should also involve a description of the kinds of activities students may pursue and should encourage questions about the program.
- *Peer Recommendation.* Look for individuals who pursue activities in or related to visual or performing arts. Often gifted individuals will share their products with peers but not with adults. For example, look for those who draw caricatures, perform in popular bands, play instruments for friends, can improvise impersonations, and so forth.
- *Tests.* Some specific areas, such as music, have tests which purport to reflect ability and potential. If these are used, they should supplement rather than supersede other sources of information.

CONCLUDING COMMENT

Some years ago a topic appeared on the Writing Sample test in English which stated, "The degree of health of a society can be measured by the extent to which it tolerates diversity." Perhaps as we consider the gifted and highly gifted in our society we would do well to remember this statement but substitute the word "encourages" or "rewards" in place of the word "tolerates." Kurt Vonnegut poses an interesting alternative in his short story "Harrison Bergeron" (17), when he asks what the world would be like if everyone were forced to be equal in every way.

Throughout this text we have suggested that in order to be able to focus upon the gifts and strengths of each individual person, a wide range of identification instruments must be used. As a teacher, as a school, as a society, can we dare to cultivate uniqueness? Can we risk being organic gardeners in our classroom rather than computer programmers, machinists, or production managers? But when we have an educational system based upon an industrial model whose stated purpose is to ensure an "efficient" operation which results in a uniform product, how can we, as teachers, find ways to remind ourselves that diversity and uniqueness are also values worth working to protect and enhance?

If we can begin to think of ourselves as gardeners, as shapers of environments rather than makers of people, perhaps we can allow each separate seed to grow and develop and maybe even flower without demanding that all the seeds do everything at the same time and in the same order. Perhaps, as we grow in our own self-understanding and self-confidence, we can begin to perceive that each seed *is* different and we can seek to enable each to become what it is and not try to force it to become something else. Perhaps we can even come to trust that the seed of strength and creativity, the source of life and health and flowering, does indeed lie deep within each person, and by so trusting we will help provide the nurturing that will call forth the seed. Who knows, in time (its own time, not necessarily ours) it may push itself upward, come into its own, and bear much fruit. What greater joy can a gardener have than to witness the variety and splendor of the living plants that responded to such careful attention?

72

References

1. Callahan, Carolyn M. *Developing Creativity in the Gifted and Talented.* Reston, Va.: Council for Exceptional Children, 1978.
2. *Education of the Gifted and Talented: Report to the Congress of the United States by the U.S. Commissioner of Education. U.S. Department of Health, Education and Welfare, Office of Education.* Washington, D.C.: Government Printing Office, 1972.
3. Forgon, Harry W. "Teachers Don't Want to Be Labeled." *Phi Delta Kappan,* September 1973.
4. Gear, Gayle. "Effects of Training in Teachers' Accuracy in Identifying Gifted Children." *Gifted Child Quarterly* 22, no. 1 (Spring 1978).
4a. Guilford, J. P. *The Nature of Human Intelligence.* New York: McGraw-Hill Book Co., 1967.
5. Jackson and Robinson. "Early Identification of Intellectually Advanced Children." Child Development Research Group, University of Washington. Paper presented at the Annual Convention of the National Association for Gifted Children, San Diego, Calif., October 1977.
6. Jacobs, J. C. "Effectiveness of Teacher and Parent Identification of Gifted Children as a Function of School Levels." *Psychology in the Schools* 8: 140–42; 1971.
7. Khatena, Joe. "Educating the Gifted Child: Challenge and Response in the U.S.A." Paper presented at the World Conference on Gifted and Talented (London, England; September 1975) and at the West Virginia Unit Association of Teacher Educators Annual Conference (Charleston, West Virginia; November 1975). ED 117 928.
8. _____. "The Gifted Child in the U.S. and Abroad." *Gifted Child Quarterly* 21: 372–87; Fall 1977.
9. Martinson, Ruth A. *The Identification of the Gifted and Talented.* Ventura, Calif.: Office of Ventura County Superintendent of Schools, 1974.
10. Moustakas, Clark E. *Creative Life.* New York: Van Nostrand Reinhold Co., 1977.
10a. New York State Education Department. *Guidelines for the Identification of the Gifted and Talented.* Albany, N.Y.: University of the State of New York, State Education Department, 1977.
11. Pegnato, Carl W., and Birch, Jack W. "Locating Gifted Children in Junior High Schools: A Comparison of Methods." *Exceptional Children* 25: 300–304; March 1959.
12. Pfleger, Lawrence R. "Research and Guidance Laboratory Practices: Identifying and Programming Gifted and Talented Students." Madison, Wisc.: University of Wisconsin, 1977. ED 138 001.
13. Renzulli, Joseph, and Smith, Linda H. "Two Approaches to Identification of Gifted Students." *Exceptional Children* 43: 512–18; May 1977.
13a. _____, and _____. *A Guidebook for Developing Individualized Educational Programs for Gifted and Talented Students.* Mansfield Center, Conn.: Creative Learning Press, 1979.
14. Skager, Rodney, and Fitzgibbon, Carol. "Mentally Gifted Disadvantaged Students: An Investigation of Methods of Identification, Including the Use of 'Culture Fair' Tests, at the English Grade Level, Final Report." Los Angeles: California University; April 1972. ED 080 583.
15. Torrance, E. Paul. "Dare We Hope Again?" *Gifted Child Quarterly* 22, no. 3; Fall, 1978.
16. Tuttle, Frederick B., Jr. *Gifted and Talented Students.* Washington, D.C.: National Education Association, 1978.
17. Vonnegut, Kurt. "Harrison Bergeron." In *Welcome to the Monkey House.* New York: Delacorte, 1968.

SUPPLEMENTARY MATERIALS

FOUR QUESTIONS

1. Is it important to identify gifted students?

Those who are planning a program for a specific group of individuals should develop a procedure to locate the students on the basis of the characteristics for which the program is designed. Formal identification depends on what the school plans to provide gifted students once they have been identified. If the school has not designed a program to promote more appropriate instruction for the identified students, then their identification does not serve any purpose other than raising the issue. Also, if the program is designed to be implemented in a heterogeneous situation, a formal identification procedure may not be necessary as the teacher may move students in and out of groups as indicated by performance. In all situations it is important to provide training for teachers so that they can locate and accommodate the gifted.

2. How should students be identified for a program?

This also depends on the goals of the school and of the particular program. In some programs the goal is to identify the top 2 percent, while in others, like Renzulli's "Revolving Door" program, the goal is to identify the top 25 percent and allow students to move in and out of the class situation on the basis of interest and "task commitment." If the aim is to locate only the gifted and not students who may not be gifted, the 2 percent model is appropriate. In such cases, the "nongifted" will certainly be excluded. However, many very gifted individuals who would benefit greatly from the program will also be excluded. Using the other extreme many "nongifted" individuals will be admitted to the program, but many very gifted individuals who would otherwise be overlooked will also be included. The number of students depends on the number that the program model can realistically accommodate. If resources are limited and the school is committed to a self-contained class per grade level, the number will probably be between 20 and 25. Many schools begin with 5 to 10 percent of the potential population and then make adjustments according to the results of the identification procedure and the parameters of the program.

3. What areas of giftedness should be stressed?

Some schools are large enough or have sufficient resources to provide for all areas. Most, however, usually begin with a few areas and, after their initial programs are well established, expand to include others. Often schools that attempt to be all things to all people soon discover that their program is too nebulous to provide adequately for any of the population. Again, the answer to this question depends on the available resources and the specific design. The resource room at the elementary level is very popular because it can provide for many areas of giftedness. Schools whose programs have a greater focus on academic areas usually find it better to select academically talented and intellectually gifted individuals and build from there. Even with the concentration on only these two areas, the program has to be diverse enough to include a wide range of different characteristics.

4. How can the identification procedure be evaluated?

Identification procedures have been evaluated in many different ways. Previously, most evaluations compared results on the identification instruments with scores on individualized IQ tests. Some recent assessments focus attention more directly on the relationship between the particular identification instruments and the specific program. By comparing instruments and even individual instrument items with performance in the specific program, these assessments can provide detailed information for modifying the procedure to locate individuals for the particular program. There are, however, two limitations of this approach: (1) the results pertain only to the particular program under investigation and should not be transferred to other, even similar, programs; (2) as the identification procedure becomes more refined for the particular program, other areas of giftedness may be overlooked to an even greater degree. If all are aware of these limitations, this approach to assessing the effectiveness of an identification procedure can be very helpful in modifying the procedure for the particular program.*

---

*Williams, Maida B.; Tuttle, Frederick B., Jr.; and Gallerani, David. "Evaluating the Effectiveness of an Identification Procedure." Unpublished report. Boston Public Schools, District III/Boston College Collaborative, 1982. And "Evaluation of Identification Procedure: Advanced Learning Activities Program." Warwick Public Schools (R.I.), 1983.

SAMPLE IDENTIFICATION INSTRUMENTS
AND MATERIALS

Although we are aware of a wide range of programs and identification procedures for gifted individuals, we, of course, do not know every one. Consequently, we have selected a few samples from those with which we are most familiar as representative of different approaches and different program goals. These approaches include a summer program for creative individuals, a full-time program for intellectually-academic gifted, and a pull-out, enrichment program for intellectually-creative gifted. Even if the specific procedure is not appropriate for your program, perhaps some of the instruments will be helpful.

The instruments most appropriate for a specific program depend on the characteristics of the population and the goals of the program. We urge you to check with your guidance counselor for materials used in the district and to examine the particular items for relevance to your program. Each school should create its own procedure, including particular instruments and specific items on inventories as well as criteria for inclusion in the program.

Performance Lists

The following checklists of behaviors of gifted individuals have been developed to help in identifying students for special programs.

Scales

Sample Items from the *Scales for Rating the Behavioral Characteristics of Superior Students**

Part I: Learning Characteristics

- Has unusually advanced vocabulary for age or grade level; uses terms in a meaningful way; has verbal behavior characterized by "richness" of expression, elaboration, and fluency.
- Possesses a large storehouse of information about a variety of topics (beyond the usual interests of youngsters his age).
- Has quick mastery and recall of factual information.

Part II: Motivational Characteristics

- Becomes absorbed and truly involved in certain topics or problems; is persistent in seeking task completion. (It is sometimes difficult to get him to move on to another topic.)
- Is easily bored with routine tasks.
- Needs little external motivation to follow through in work that initially excites him.

Part III: Creativity Characteristics

- Displays a great deal of curiosity about many things; is constantly asking questions about anything and everything.
- Generates a large number of ideas or solutions to problems and questions; often offers unusual ("way out"), unique, clever responses.
- Is uninhibited in expressions of opinion; is sometimes radical and spirited in disagreement; is tenacious.

Part IV: Leadership Characteristics

- Carries responsibility well; can be counted on to do what he has promised and usually does it well.
- Is self-confident with children his own age as well as adults; seems comfortable when asked to show his work to the class.
- Seems to be well liked by his classmates.

Part V: Artistic Characteristics

- Likes to participate in art activities; is eager to visually express ideas.
- Incorporates a large number of elements into art work; varies the subject and content of art work.
- Arrives at unique, unconventional solutions to artistic problems as opposed to traditional, conventional ones.

Part VI: Musical Characteristics

- Shows a sustained interest in music— seeks out opportunities to hear and create music.
- Perceives fine differences in musical tone (pitch, loudness, timbre, duration).
- Easily remembers melodies and can produce them accurately.

Part VII: Dramatics Characteristics

- Volunteers to participate in classroom plays or skits.
- Easily tells a story or gives an account of some experience.
- Effectively uses gestures and facial expressions to communicate feelings.

Part VIII: Communication Characteristics— Precision

- Speaks and writes directly and to the point.
- Modifies and adjusts expression of ideas for maximum reception.
- Is able to revise and edit in a way which is concise, yet retains essential ideas.

Part IX: Communication Characteristics— Expressiveness

- Uses voice expressively to convey or enhance meaning.
- Conveys information nonverbally through gestures, facial expressions, and "body language."
- Is an interesting storyteller.

Part X: Planning Characteristics

- Determines what information or resources are necessary for accomplishing a task.
- Grasps the relationship of individual steps to the whole process.
- Allows time to execute all steps involved in a process.

* From **A Guidebook for Developing Individualized Educational Programs for Gifted and Talented Students**, by Joseph S. Renzulli and Linda H. Smith (Mansfield Center, Conn.: Creative Learning Press, 1979), Figure 2 (p. 7).

Teacher Checklists*

Checklist for Kindergarten Students

Student's Name _____ School _____ Date _____

DIRECTIONS: Please place an X on the line beside each question which **BEST** describes the student.

	NO	YES
A. LANGUAGE		
1. Is the pupil able to read above grade level 1.5?	___	___
2. Indicate grade level for independent reading comprehension.	___	
3. Does the pupil understand the relationship of such words as up—down, top—bottom, big—little, far—near?	___	___
4. Does the pupil follow a three-step direction?	___	___
5. Does the pupil remain on task for a minimum of 25 minutes?	___	___
B. PSYCHOMOTOR ABILITIES		
1. Can the pupil skip, throw, and catch?	___	___
2. Does the pupil exhibit coordination by being able to bounce a ball or tie shoelaces?	___	___
3. Can the pupil reproduce a five-beat rhythm pattern?	___	___
4. Can the pupil draw a person? **Please attach example.**	___	___
5. Can the pupil complete the missing parts of an incomplete familiar picture by drawing the parts in their proper perspective?	___	___
6. Can the pupil reproduce a three-dimensional design?	___	___
7. Can the pupil hear likenesses and differences in the beginnings of words; e.g., hill-bill, feet-treat, boat-coat?	___	___
C. MATHEMATICS		
1. Can the pupil repeat five digits forward and three reversed?	___	___
2. Can the pupil join and separate a sequence of sets?	___	___
3. Can the pupil recognize and understand the value of coins (penny, nickle, dime, and quarter)?	___	___

* Checklists for Kindergarten Students, First Grade Students, and Grades 2–6 are from materials prepared for Dade County (Florida) Public Schools, James S. Miley, Coordinator for the Gifted.

78

	Seldom or Never	Occasionally	Frequently	Almost always

D. CREATIVITY

1. Can the pupil interpret stories or pictures in his own words?
2. Can the pupil predict possible outcomes for a story?
3. Can the pupil create rhymes which communicate?
4. Does the pupil offer solutions for problems that are discussed in the classroom?
5. Does the pupil display curiosity by asking many questions or by other types of behavior?
6. Does the pupil question critically?
7. Does the pupil explore new ideas or invent new ways of saying and telling?

E. GENERAL CHARACTERISTICS

1. Does the pupil readily adapt to new situations; is he flexible in thought and action; and does he seem undisturbed when the normal routine is changed?
2. Does the pupil seek new tasks and activities?
3. Is the pupil cooperative; does he tend to avoid bickering; and is he generally easy to get along with?
4. Does the pupil tend to dominate others and generally direct the activity in which he is involved?
5. Does the pupil appear to be happy and well adjusted in school work, as evidenced by relaxed attitude, self-confidence, and pride in work?

Checklist for First Grade Students

Student's Name _____ School _____ Date _____

DIRECTIONS: Please place an X on the line beside each question which **BEST** describes the student.

	NO	YES
1. Is the pupil able to read two years above grade?	___	___
2. Indicate grade level for independent reading comprehension.	___	
3. Can the pupil recognize the number and sequence of steps in a specified direction?	___	___
4. Can the pupil recognize the properties of right angles in a geometric figure?	___	___
5. Can the pupil identify a three-dimensional object from a two-dimensional projection and/or a two-dimensional object from a three-dimensional projection?	___	___
6. Does the pupil form sets and subsets?	___	___
7. Does the pupil understand the concepts of place value?	___	___

8. Can the pupil create a short story for a familiar subject?
9. Can the pupil interpret stories and pictures in his own words?
10. Does the pupil display curiosity by asking questions about anything and everything?
11. Does the pupil question critically?
12. Does the pupil demonstrate flexibility in his thinking pattern and the ability to communicate this to others?
13. Does the pupil perform independently?
14. Can the pupil complete the missing parts of an incomplete familiar picture by drawing the parts in their proper perspective?
15. Does the pupil exhibit superior ability in performing in an organized physical activity and obeying the rules?
16. Does the pupil make associations between sounds and their symbols?
17. Does the pupil tend to dominate others and generally direct the activity in which he is involved?
18. Does the pupil appear to be happy and well adjusted in school work, as evidenced by relaxed attitude, self-confidence, and pride in work?
19. Does the pupil demonstrate tendencies to organize people, things, and situations?
20. Does the pupil follow through with tasks that initially he was motivated to do?
21. Does the pupil readily adapt to new situations; is he flexible in thought and action; and does he seem undisturbed when the normal routine is changed?
22. Does the pupil seek new tasks and activities?
23. Is the pupil cooperative; does he tend to avoid bickering; and is he generally easy to get along with?
24. Is the pupil self-confident with pupils his own age and/or adults; seems comfortable when asked to show his work to the class?

80

RATING SCALE #1: PUPIL LEARNING CHARACTERISTICS

Student's Name _____ School _____ Date _____

DIRECTIONS: Please place an X on the line beside
each question which **BEST** describes the
student.

	Seldom or Never	Occa- sionally	Fre- quently	Almost always
1. Has verbal behavior characterized by "richness: of expression and elaboration."	___	___	___	___
2. Possesses a large storehouse of information about a variety of topics beyond the usual interests of youngsters his age.	___	___	___	___
3. Has rapid insight into cause-effect relationships; tries to discover the how and why of things; asks many provocative questions; wants to know what makes things or people "tick."	___	___	___	___
4. Has a ready grasp of underlying principles and can quickly make valid generalizations about events, people or things; looks for similarities and differences.	___	___	___	___
5. Is a keen and alert observer; usually "sees more" or "gets more" out of a story, film, etc., than others.	___	___	___	___
6. Reads a great deal on his own; does not avoid difficult material; may show a preference for biography, autobiography, encyclopedias, atlases, travel, folk tales, poetry, science, history, and drama.	___	___	___	___

7. Tries to understand complicated material by
separating it into its respective parts; reasons
things out for himself; sees logical and common
sense answers.
8. Is the pupil achieving two years above grade level in reading? Grade Level _____
9. Is the pupil achieving two years above grade level in mathematics? Grade Level _____

RATING SCALE #2: PUPIL MOTIVATIONAL CHARACTERISTICS

Student's Name _____ School _____ Date _____

DIRECTIONS: Please place an X on the line beside each question which **BEST** describes the student.

	Seldom or Never	Occa-sionally	Fre-quently	Almost always
1. Becomes absorbed and truly involved in certain topics or problems; is persistent in seeking task completion—sometimes it is difficult to get him to move on to another topic.	____	____	____	____
2. Is easily bored with routine tasks.	____	____	____	____
3. Follows through with tasks that initially he was motivated to do.	____	____	____	____
4. Is self-critical; strives toward perfection.	____	____	____	____
5. Prefers to work independently; needs minimal direction from teachers.	____	____	____	____
6. Is positive and zealous in his beliefs.	____	____	____	____
7. Has tendency to organize people, things, and situations.	____	____	____	____
8. Is concerned with right and wrong, good and bad; often evaluates and passes judgment on events, people, and things.	____	____	____	____

RATING SCALE #3: CREATIVITY CHARACTERISTICS

Student's Name _____ School _____ Date _____

	Seldom or Never	Occa-sionally	Fre-quently	Almost always

DIRECTIONS: Please place an X on the line beside each question which **BEST** describes the student.

	Seldom or Never	Occa-sionally	Fre-quently	Almost always
1. Displays curiosity about many things; is constantly asking questions about anything and everything.	____	____	____	____
2. Generates a large number of ideas or solutions to problems and questions; often offers unusual, "way out," unique, clever responses.	____	____	____	____
3. Is uninhibited in expressions of opinion; is sometimes radical and spirited in disagreement; is tenacious.	____	____	____	____
4. Is a high risk taker; is adventurous and speculative.	____	____	____	____

	Seldom or Never	Occa-sionally	Fre-quently	Almost always

5. Displays a good deal of intellectual playfulness; fantasizes; imagines; manipulates ideas—changes, elaborates upon them.

6. Displays a keen sense of humor and sees humor in situations that may not appear to be humorous to others.

7. Is unusually aware of his impulses and more open to the irrational in himself.

8. Is sensitive to beauty; responds to aesthetic characteristics of things.

9. Is nonconforming; is not interested in details; is individualistic; does not fear being different.

10. Criticizes constructively; is unwilling to accept authoritarian pronouncements without critical examination.

RATING SCALE #4: LEADERSHIP CHARACTERISTICS

Student's Name _____ School _____ Date _____

	Seldom or Never	Occa-sionally	Fre-quently	Almost always

DIRECTIONS: Please place an X on the line beside each question which **BEST** describes the student.

1. Carries responsibility well; follows through with tasks and usually does them well.

2. Is self-confident with children his own age as well as adults; seems comfortable when asked to show his work to the class.

3. Seems to be respected by his classmates.

4. Is cooperative with teacher and classmates; tends to avoid bickering and is generally easy to get along with.

5. Can express himself well; has good verbal facility and is usually well understood.

6. Adapts readily to new situations; is flexible in thought and action and does not seem disturbed when the normal routine is changed.

7. Seems to enjoy being around other people, is sociable, and prefers not to be alone.

8. Tends to dominate others when they are around; generally directs the activity in which he is involved.

9. Participates in most activities connected with the school; can be depended upon to be there.

Checklist for Middle Grades and Above*

Student's Name   School   Grade   Homeroom

Teacher's Name   School Term

To the Teachers:

We need your help. We're looking for children in your classroom who you feel might be more able than their test scores indicate. The following list of characteristics, while by no means all inclusive, represents traits found in gifted and creative children. If any student in your class is described by at least twelve (12) of the items on this list, you may want to watch him more carefully for possible inclusion in the gifted program. Those items which are **most** applicable should be double checked. Will you help us by responding to the following checklist for the top students in your class? Supporting information and comments should be written on the back of this form.

1. Is an avid reader.
2. Has received an award in science, art, literature.
3. Has avid interest in science or literature.
4. Very alert, rapid answers.
5. Is outstanding in math.
6. Has a wide range of interests.
7. Is very secure emotionally.
8. Is venturesome, anxious to do new things.
9. Tends to dominate peers or situations.
10. Readily makes money on various projects or activities—is an entrepreneur.
11. Individualistic—likes to work by self.
12. Is sensitive to feelings of others—or to situations.
13. Has confidence in self.
14. Needs little outside control—disciplines self.
15. Adept at visual art expression.
16. Resourceful—can solve problems by ingenious methods.
17. Creative in thoughts, new ideas, seeing associations, innovations, etc. (not artistically).
18. Body or facial gestures very expressive.
19. Impatient—quick to anger or anxious to complete a task.
20. Great desire to excel even to the point of cheating.
21. Colorful verbal expressions.
22. Tells very imaginative stories.
23. Frequently interrupts others when they are talking.
24. Frank in appraisal of adults.
25. Has mature sense of humor (puns, associations, etc.).
26. Is inquisitive.
27. Takes a close look at things.
28. Is eager to tell others about discoveries.
29. Can show relationships among apparently unrelated ideas.
30. Shows excitement in voice about discoveries.
31. Has a tendency to lose awareness of time.

---

* From San Francisco Unified School District Programs for Mentally Gifted Minors, William B. Cummings, Supervisor.

Student's Name _____

Last   First   Initial   School   Date

Please check the column which best describes student.	Truly Exceptional—Highest 5%	Outstanding—Highest 5%	Excellent—Next Highest 15%	Good—Next Highest 15%	Above Average—Next 15%	Average—Middle 20%	Poor—Lowest 40%
Initiative: Carries responsibility well; follows through with tasks and usually does them well. Is positive and zealous in beliefs; is self-critical, striving to do better.							
Courage: Is a high risk taker; is adventurous and speculative.							
Self-Confidence: Is self-confident with students his own age as well as adults; seems comfortable when asked to show his work to the class.							
Curiosity: Tries to discover how and why of things; asks many provocative questions.							
Independence: A—Prefers to work independently; needs minimal direction.							
B—Generally directs the activity in which he is involved.							
Health: Good health; attendance and tardiness not a factor in grading.							
Responsibility: Can follow written and oral directions, stays on task, handles equipment.							
Flexibility: Adapts readily to new situations; is flexible in thought and action.							
Expressiveness: Can express himself well; has good verbal facility and is usually well understood; has ability to organize ideas in written form.							
Respect for Others: Is cooperative with teacher and peers; tends to avoid bickering and is generally easy to get along with.							

If you know of some particular reason why this student **should** or **should not** be in the Program, please comment on opposite side.

Teacher's Name _____ Subject _____ Date _____

* From materials prepared for Dade County (Florida) Public Schools, James S. Miley, Coordinator for the Gifted.

Checklist for Culturally Disadvantaged Underachieving Mentally Gifted Minors
(Suggested by the State Consultants in the Education of the Mentally Gifted)*

1. Early evidence of:
   _____ School-related learning
   _____ Maturation
   _____ Active and persistent exploration of environment
   _____ Imitation of adult behavior
   _____ Questioning of established ways of doing things or of assignments and directions

2. Unusually resourceful in coping with:

   2.1 Responsibilities
   _____ Home
   _____ School
   _____ Work
   _____ Community
   _____ Other

   2.2 Opportunities
   _____ Access to resources
   _____ Free and/or unstructured time
   _____ New environments
   _____ New experiences
   _____ Other

   2.3 Deprivations
   _____ Economic
   _____ Social
   _____ Expression, information, planning,
           communication, exploration
   _____ Cultural
   _____ Educational

   2.4 Problems, Frustrations, and Obstacles
   _____ School
   _____ Home
   _____ Social
   _____ Other

   2.5 Lack of Structure and Direction
   _____ No closure
   _____ Poor or irrational organization of:
           _____ Time
           _____ Work tasks
           _____ Learning experiences
           _____ Social experiences

   2.6 Overly structured settings
   _____ With no or few opportunities to
           explore alternatives
   _____ With overemphasis on rigid
           expectations and with rigid role
           performance
   _____ With no or few opportunities to do
           things in new ways

3. Playful with:
   _____ Materials
   _____ People (interpersonal relations)
   _____ Ideas
   _____ Other things

4. Sense of humor (Describe)

* Obtained through Dr. Paul Plowman, California State Department of Education.

5. Products (List)

6. Achievements (List)

7. Skills (List)

8. Scores on intellectual ability tests:
   _____ Scores compared with norms for culturally disadvantaged children
   _____ Nonverbal score as compared with verbal score

9. Intelligence/achievement scattergram profiles and aptitude test scores

10. Ratings on maturation profiles; e.g., Gesell

Name _____ Date _____

School _____ Grade _____ Age _____

Able disadvantaged pupils evidence superior ability in one or more of the five areas listed below. No pupil is expected to demonstrate ability in all areas, but an analysis of strengths may indicate potential. It is important to note that these characteristics can be evidenced in both positive and negative ways and either manifestation is an indicator of strength. Examples of negative indicators have been enclosed in parenthesis.

The classroom teacher who works daily with pupils is best qualified to make these observations. Place an **X** on the line beside each statement which **BEST** describes this pupil. If the behavior has not been observed, leave the line blank.

	YES	NO
A. LEARNING		
• Demonstrates verbal proficiency in small group problem-solving tasks.	____	____
• Has unusually advanced vocabulary for age or grade level.	____	____
• Has verbal behavior characterized by "richness" of expression, imagery, elaboration, and fluency in any language. (Sometimes rambles on and on.)	____	____
• Possesses a large storehouse of information about a variety of topics beyond the usual interests of age peers.	____	____
• Has rapid insight into cause-effect relationships; tries to discover the how and why of things; asks many provocative questions; wants to know what makes things or people "tick." (Can be an annoyance in persisting to ask questions.)	____	____
• Has a ready grasp of underlying principles; can quickly make valid generalizations about events, people or things. (Sometimes skeptical.)	____	____
• Looks for similarities and differences.	____	____
• Reads independently; does not avoid difficult material; may show a preference for biography, autobiography, encyclopedia, atlases, travel, folk tales, poetry, science, history, and drama.	____	____
• Tries to understand complicated material by separating it into its respective parts; reasons things out and sees logical and common sense answers.	____	____
• Catches on quickly; retains and uses new ideas and information.	____	____
• Has a facility for learning English if bilingual.	____	____
• Is a keen and alert observer; usually "sees more" or "gets more" out of a story, film, etc., than others.	____	____
B. MOTIVATION		
• Evidences power of concentration.	____	____
• Prefers to work independently with minimal direction from teachers. (Resists directions.)	____	____
• Has tendency to organize people, things, and situations. (Resists opinions of others; wants own way.)	____	____
• Is concerned with right and wrong, good and bad. (Makes decisions with little tolerance for shades of "grey.")	____	____

---

* From materials prepared by Los Angeles Unified School District.

- Takes advantage of opportunities to learn and enjoys challenge. _____ _____
- Is self-critical and strives for perfection. (Sometimes critical of others and not self.) _____ _____
- Often is self-assertive. (Can be stubbornly set in ideas.) _____ _____
- Requires little drill to grasp concepts; seeks other than routine tasks. (Needs to know reasons for activity.) _____ _____
- Becomes absorbed and involved in certain topics or problems. _____ _____
- Is persistent in task completion. (Sometimes unwilling to change tasks.) _____ _____
- Likes structure and order but not static procedures. (Is frustrated by lack of progress.) _____ _____
- Is motivated by sports, music, and concrete subjects. _____ _____

C. LEADERSHIP

- Accepts and carries responsibility; follows through with tasks and usually does them well. _____ _____
- Is self-confident with age peers; is usually well understood by them. (Can be self-assertive and dominant.) _____ _____
- Seems well liked by classmates and is looked upon as a leader. (Needs peer approval and acceptance.) _____ _____
- Shows developing understanding in how to relate to teachers and classmates. (Sometimes has a rebellious attitude.) _____ _____
- Tends to dominate others and generally organizes and directs activities when involved in a group. _____ _____
- Adapts readily to new situations; is flexible in thought and actions and is not disturbed when normal routine is changed. _____ _____
- Seems to enjoy being with other people; is sociable and prefers not to be alone. (Sometimes is a loner.) _____ _____
- Takes initiative and shows independence of action. _____ _____
- Is a social leader on playground and off campus. _____ _____

D. CREATIVITY

- Displays intellectual playfulness; fantasizes; imagines; manipulates ideas by elaboration or modification. _____ _____
- Is a high risk taker; is adventurous and speculative. (Has different criteria for success.) _____ _____
- Displays a keen sense of humor reflective of own cultural background. _____ _____
- Is individualistic; does not fear being different. (Departs from peer norm in action and behavior.) _____ _____
- Predicts from present information. _____ _____
- Displays a curiosity about many things; has many hobbies. _____ _____
- Generates a large number of ideas or solutions to problems and questions. _____ _____
- Responds emotionally to stories, events, and needs of others. _____ _____
- Shows ability in oral expression. _____ _____
- Demonstrates exceptional ability in written expression; creates stories, plays, etc. _____ _____
- Is sensitive to color, design, arrangement and other qualities showing artistic appreciation and understanding. _____ _____
- Is sensitive to melody, rhythm, form, tonal coloring, mood, and other qualities showing music appreciation. _____ _____
- Demonstrates exceptional ability in one of the fine arts (underline area of strength): dancing, painting/drawing, sculpturing/clay modeling, instrumental or vocal music, role-playing/drama. _____ _____

	YES	NO

- Demonstrates unusual ability in one of the practical arts (underline area of strength): handicrafts, wood, metal, print, design, mechanics. _____ _____
- Demonstrates exceptional skill and ability in physical coordination activities. _____ _____
- Shows interest in unconventional careers. _____ _____
- Improvises with commonplace materials. _____ _____

E. ADAPTABILITY

- Handles outside responsibilities and meets school demands. _____ _____
- Learns through experience and is flexible and resourceful in solving day-to-day problems. _____ _____
- Deals effectively with deprivations, problems, frustrations, or obstacles caused by the complexities of living conditions. _____ _____
- Overcomes lack of environmental structure and direction. (Needs emotional support and sympathetic attitude.) _____ _____
- Displays high degree of social reasoning and/or behavior and shows ability to discriminate. _____ _____
- Uses limited resources to make meaningful products. _____ _____
- Displays maturity of judgment and reasoning beyond own age level. _____ _____
- Is knowledgeable about things of which others are unaware. _____ _____
- Can transfer learning from one situation to another. _____ _____

Questionnaires and Inventories

The following materials have been developed to obtain information from a variety of sources, including parents, peers, and the candidate. They should, of course, be modified for each particular program and situation.

Self

Self-Portrait*

Self-expression has many forms and holds a significant place in each of our lives. We encourage you to ponder and share the exploration of yourself with us through a self-portrait. Rather than showing how you appear to others, express yourself as you feel yourself to be. Your self-portrait may be a symbol or image or any combination of line, shape, and color that stands for you.

After you have completed your self-portrait on a separate piece of paper, write a brief interpretation of it in the space below.

The "openness" of this task may lead to some valuable insights not obtainable elsewhere.

---

* From Horizons Unlimited, Keene State College, Keene, N. H.

Autobiographical Questionnaire*

Name _____ Student _____ Teacher _____

Address _____ Age _____

_____

Telephone _____

Please approach the following questions from an autobiographical point-of-view. Skip any questions you prefer not to answer. All questionnaires will be completely confidential.

1. What occupation do you have or do you envisage? For what reasons did you choose the work you are doing or planning?

2. Have any particular cultural works held deep meaning for you (e.g., books, films, music, theatre, painting, etc.) and how were you affected by them?

3. How would you describe the quality of your relationships with other people, including strong and weak points? How would these affect your participation in a living-learning situation with 40 other people for 4 weeks?

4. What significance and value has friendship for you?

5. What events, activities, and inner conditions have given you the most satisfaction and joy? Which have made you suffer most? Which have had most meaning and significance for you?

6. Are there any values and ideals which you hold firmly as a result of your own experience? How do you express these in your life? How do you fail to express them?

7. What is your perception of education? How do you think you learn best?

8. What is your opinion about the present epoch in human history and consciousness? In what ways do you think we are making progress or losing ground? What do you see as the major challenges facing mankind today?

These questions relate specifically to the philosophy of Horizons Unlimited. Your questions should reflect your philosophy.

---

* From Horizons Unlimited, Keene State College, Keene, N. H.

92

Biographical Inventory*

1. Academic Achievement
   How fast do you learn new material in school, compared with others your age?
   A. Much faster than most
   B. Just a little faster than most
   C. About the same as most
   D. Just a little slower than most

2. Creativity
   How often do you read an advanced text to learn more about a subject of interest to you?
   A. Not very often
   B. About once or twice a month
   C. About once a week
   D. A few times a week
   E. Once a day or more

3. Artistic Potential
   Do you like to practice to develop your talent or skill in a particular artistic or musical activity?
   A. Yes
   B. Sometimes
   C. No

4. Leadership
   How much time do you spend in organized school activities (plays, band, student government, etc.)?
   A. Most of my spare time
   B. Quite a bit
   C. Some
   D. Very little
   E. None

5. Vocational Maturity
   Do you know what kinds of education or training are necessary for certain jobs?
   A. Have not really thought about this question.
   B. I know some of the kinds of schooling or training needed.
   C. I know what kinds of education or training are needed for the jobs I'm considering.

6. Educational Orientation
   How long do you expect to go to school?
   A. Only until I can quit
   B. Until I graduate from high school
   C. Some schooling after high school
   D. Until I graduate from college
   E. Don't know

---

* Sample items from *Biographical Inventory: Form U*, Institute for Behavioral Resources in Creativity (IBRIC), Salt Lake City, Utah, 1976.

Parent Questionnaire*
Examiner Instructions

1. Don't tell the parent this is a questionnaire to determine if the child will be called "gifted" and put in a special program. It isn't!

2. Some parents are more verbal than others. Some parents will go to great lengths to fill out a written questionnaire, others don't like to write anything and will respond Yes, No. Write down any anecdotes the parent *tells* about the child, whether the story seems relevant or not. The more information we get, the better.

Questioner assessment: Do you think the parent gave information comfortably?

Did it seem *to you* that the parent overestimated or underestimated the child's abilities?

This questionnaire could be used by any teacher to help instruction—an important point.

Some parents fear the school setting and this should be taken into account when reading reports. Lack of response from parent does *not* indicate lack of ability.

---

* By Margot Nicholas Parrot for the Bucksport/Orland Gifted Task Force, June 1978.

Parent Questionnaire

We are trying to find out your child's special strengths. Please be as accurate as possible—do not overestimate or underestimate. Any personal stories that you wish to share with us will help us to better understand your child. There is a space after most questions for your remarks. If you want extra paper, or if you would rather tell a story than write it, please let the questioner know. You may also want to give the questioner a sample of your child's art work or a story he/she has made up.

Note lack of reference to special program or "gifted" ability.

Child's name:

Parent(s):

Address:

School or preschool program if any:

Child's birthdate:

What sports or dance experience has your child had, formally or informally (such as family games, swimming lessons, etc.)?

Note use of "fill-in" responses when appropriate.

How does the child compare with other children of the same age in physical activities?

At what physical activities is he/she especially good or especially slow?

Does the child have any physical handicaps that you know of or suspect?

At what age did your child learn to do these things:

	Age	Not Yet	Don't Know
Cut out pictures with scissors.			
Color within the lines.			
Tie shoes.			
Print alphabet letters.			
Print name or other words·			
Write out or copy stories/poems.			

Does your child excel at art? What kind?

Does your child play a musical instrument? What?

How often does the child use materials like clay or playdough, crayons, paper, paints, paste, etc., at home?

When did your child start doing these things:

	Age	Not Yet	Don't Know
Name alphabet letters (in books, on signs).			
Read/spell own name.			
Read individual word(s).			
Read simple books (like *Hop on Pop*).			
Read harder books (by him/herself).			
Count to 20.			
Do addition (subtraction) in head (or with objects or on fingers).			
Tell time.			
Count money.			
Remember phone number.			

Does the child understand ideas that seem too complicated for a young child? Like what?

Does he/she use big words or talk in long sentences?

Does the child have an unusually long attention span, or does he/she spend a long time doing any one activity, especially a favorite one?

Does he/she have a special sense of fairness, of justice?

Does he/she have an unusually good memory?

Are there any intellectual or school-type activities at which your child is better than most? What?

Does this child have any known or *suspected* mental or perceptual handicaps? Describe:

(Creativity)
Does the child make up stories, songs, or poems? Are they unusual?

Does the child act out stories or plays with his/her body or with puppets or toys? With other children? Describe:

Does your child come up with unusual excuses for not doing things?

Does he/she have a vivid imagination? Explain:

(Leadership)
How does the child get along with these people:

Question	Very Well	Normal—O.K.	Not Well
Kids of his/her age			
Adults			
Older children			
Younger children			
Large groups			
Small groups (2–4 kids)			

When playing games or getting into mischief, is this child often the leader?

Does he/she prefer to play alone _____, or in small groups _____, or the more the better _____?

Has he/she ever been with a group of kids regularly (like nursery school, church group, etc.)? Describe:

How did she/he like it?

(Family/general)
What are the child's favorite activities?

What are the family's favorite activities?

Every parent sees special things about his/her child that other people miss. Describe your child:

Peer Referral Form*

Your Name _____ Person Being Referred _____

Date _____ Grade _____

Answer the following questions as candidly and accurately as possible. Feel free to use the back of this sheet or an additional sheet if necessary.

1. In what capacity do you know the person you are referring? How long have you known him/her?

2. What things about this person led you to think he/she would be a candidate for Project Discovery?

3. Do you see this person as someone who can work independently on something or some project? If left on his/her own, could this person be expected to complete his/her work?

4. In what way is this person creative? For example, could the student interest people around him/her with an original story? Could he/she be bored? Could the person be relied on to come up with something unique and unusual in school or outside of school? A "yes" answer to any of these questions or many others could suggest the person be creative.

5. Is this person organized in his/her work or recreation? Some questions you might ask yourself are: Would I benefit in planning my own project with this person's help? If I gave this student something he/she was capable of doing, would he/she get the job done?

This item may be seen as too much work.

There are a lot of questions in this one item. Could some be a checklist or "fill in the blank"?

* From Project Discovery, Oak Hill High School, Wales, Maine.

99

Peer Identification—Creativity—Elementary*

Pretend our class found a puppy on the playground.

A. Which three students would be most likely to think up lots of names for the puppy?

1. _____ 2. _____ 3. _____

Which three would make up the *most unusual* names?

1. _____ 2. _____ 3. _____

Which three would think of names no one else would think of?

1. _____ 2. _____ 3. _____

Which three probably would come up with the name we would finally decide on?

1. _____ 2. _____ 3. _____

B. Which three students would be most likely to write a story about the puppy?

1. _____ 2. _____ 3. _____

C. Which three students would probably think up *different* ways to teach the puppy a trick?

1. _____ 2. _____ 3. _____

D. If we design a collar for our puppy, which three students would probably come up with the *most* designs for a collar?

1. _____ 2. _____ 3. _____

the *fanciest* collar?

1. _____ 2. _____ 3. _____

the most *unusual* collar?

1. _____ 2. _____ 3. _____

E. Which three students would make the most suggestions of what could be done with the puppy?

1. _____ 2. _____ 3. _____

F. Which three would give the teacher the most reasons for allowing the dog to come into the classroom?

1. _____ 2. _____ 3. _____

---

* From *Ideas for Identification of Gifted Children in the Area of Creativity,* Franklin County Region 7, Area Service Center for Educators of Gifted Children, Marion, Illinois.

Peer Identification—Creativity—Secondary*

Think about the students in our class. Answer the following questions as completely as possible.

Which three students are the most curious about many things?

1. _____ 2. _____ 3. _____

have the most ideas and solutions to problems?

1. _____ 2. _____ 3. _____

don't seem to care what others think about what they say?

1. _____ 2. _____ 3. _____

like to take chances?

1. _____ 2. _____ 3. _____

have the most fun imagining about situations and things?

1. _____ 2. _____ 3. _____

are most sensitive to the feelings and concerns of others?

1. _____ 2. _____ 3. _____

have the best sense of humor?

1. _____ 2. _____ 3. _____

are aware of and enjoy beautiful things?

1. _____ 2. _____ 3. _____

are not concerned with details?

1. _____ 2. _____ 3. _____

do not care if others think of them as being different?

1. _____ 2. _____ 3. _____

are real individuals?

1. _____ 2. _____ 3. _____

are apt to question authority?

1. _____ 2. _____ 3. _____

---

* From *Ideas for Identification of Gifted Children in the Area of Creativity,* Franklin County Region 7, Area Service Center for Educators of Gifted Children, Marion, Illinois.

*Recommendation Form**

Recommendation for _____
(Name of Applicant)

Horizons Unlimited is a summer program for gifted adolescents and teachers. We are looking for young people who show extraordinary learning ability and/or high creative potential in the areas of: intellectual ability and academic aptitude, the visual and performing arts, problem solving, leadership and social relationships, craftsmanship (woodwork, metalwork, etc.). They may also have a high degree of insight into themselves and others. We would like you to give us information about this candidate that we cannot get elsewhere. What do you see in this person?

Recommended by _____ Date _____
(Signature)

_____
(Address)

Relationship to Applicant _____
(peer, teacher, counselor, etc.)

Note the description of the program. It will help the writer to highlight particular activities and achievements.

* From Horizons Unlimited, Keene State College, Keene, N. H.

Referral Form

Teacher-Community Member Referral Form*

NAME _____ POSITION IN COMMUNITY/SCHOOL _____

STUDENT BEING REFERRED _____

_____ DATE OF REFERRAL _____

Answer the following questions as candidly and accurately as possible. Feel free to use the back of this sheet if necessary.

1. In what capacity have you known the student? Describe fully your relationship with him/her. For how long have you known the student?

2. What characteristics of the student led you to recommend him/her for Project Discovery?

3. Cite examples of the student's ability to work independently in your contact with him/her. Be specific as to nature and difficulty of such independently offered or assigned work.

4. Cite examples of the student's ability to think creatively or to be creative which might suggest a gifted or talented potential.

5. Cite examples of the student's ability to be organized in his/her thinking or work production.

6. Cite examples of the student's commitment to long-term projects or concepts. Is he/she consistent in such commitment? If so, how is such consistency demonstrated?

7. In your opinion how is, or how has the student a potential to be, an asset to your school/community?

Please complete the following checklist by circling the number which best represents the way you view the student. Give an accurate estimate of the student's makeup. Low scores in some areas may not be negative considering the overall picture you have given of the student.

WORKS WELL IN A GROUP	(low)	1 2 3 4 5	(high)
INQUISITIVENESS	(low)	1 2 3 4 5	(high)
AMBITION	(low)	1 2 3 4 5	(high)
LEADERSHIP	(low)	1 2 3 4 5	(high)
ACADEMIC ACHIEVEMENT	(low)	1 2 3 4 5	(high)
ABILITY TO CONCEPTUALIZE	(low)	1 2 3 4 5	(high)

Some of this form could have been "fill in the blank" to separate different kinds of information.

Some indication of the characteristics pertinent to this program would help.

Sometimes items contain too many questions.

Note the reminders of which number is high and which is low.

* From Project Discovery, Oak Hill High School, Wales, Maine.

Student Application Form*

Name _____ Birth Date _____
        Last   First   Middle   Da/Mo/Yr

Home Address _____ Telephone _____

School Address _____ Telephone _____

Sex ___ Male ___ Female   Social Security Number _____

Present Grade Level 9th ___ 10th ___ 11th ___ 12th ___

Parents' Name _____

Parents' Address _____ Telephone _____

If not living with your parents, give name and address of person with whom you live:

_____

_____

Parents' Work Address(es) _____

_____ Telephone _____

In Case of Emergency, contact: _____

_____ Telephone _____

School Subjects of Major Interest _____

Interests Outside of School _____

_____

Future Plans Beyond High School _____

_____

The following information is *necessary* to complete your Horizons application:

1. Questionnaire (enclosed)
2. *High School transcript* (Have your school mail it directly to Horizons Unlimited, Keene State College, Keene, N.H. 03431)
3. Three written recommendations—*one from a peer, two from teachers, counselors, clergy or other interested adults (non-relatives)*. Recommendation forms are enclosed.
4. Self-portrait (instructions are enclosed)
5. Registration fee of $20.00. This is part of the total program cost and will be refunded only if you are not selected for the program.

It is a good idea to list the necessary forms as a help to the applicant. A checklist could be made.

* From Horizons Unlimited, Keene State College, Keene, N.H.

Creativity Measures

The following are excerpts from creativity tests and questionnaires to help teachers identify creatively gifted and talented individuals.

Talent Survey Form*

You have talents. Your friends, parents or teachers know about some of them. Some only you know. Please list below what you feel to be your talents. Put a check mark by those talents other people know about in the column so marked. Also put a check next to the talent only you know about in the column marked "No One Else Knows About It."

NAME: _____

TALENT I KNOW I HAVE	OTHER PEOPLE KNOW ABOUT IT	NO ONE ELSE KNOWS ABOUT IT
1.		
2.		
3.		
4.		
5.		
6.		
7.		
8.		
9.		
10.		
11.		
12.		

"Talent" might have been defined a little more, perhaps with an example.

The last column alerts the student to the applicability of talents outside school.

* From Greece Central School District, Greece, N.Y.

Creativity Tests

E. Paul Torrance has described several activities to help determine an individual's creative ability. Examples of these activities follow.*

Ask-and-Guess

One of the clearest and most straightforward models of the creative thinking process is found in the Ask-and-Guess Test, of which there are several different forms. In all forms, subjects are shown a picture and given the following series of instructions:

Asking questions

The next three tasks will give you a chance to see how good you are at asking questions to find out things that you do not know and in making guesses about possible causes and consequences of events. Look at the picture. What is happening? What can you tell for sure? What do you need to know to understand what is happening, what caused it to happen, and what will be the result?

Young children are asked to dictate their responses to an adult, and older children and adults are asked to write theirs. In the written version, the following instructions are given for the first of the three tasks:

On this page, write out all of the questions you can think of about the picture on the page before this one. Ask all of the questions you would need to ask to know for sure what is happening. Do not ask questions that can be answered just by looking at the drawing.

The reader who would like to test himself can get a sheet of paper and respond to the foregoing instructions with the stimulus picture, Figure 1. The time limit for the regular test is five minutes but for this demonstrator form it is three minutes. At the end of this article there is a list of the *common* responses carrying a score of zero.

Figure 1

* Excerpted from "Examples and Rationales of Test Tasks for Assessing Creative Abilities" by E. Paul Torrance in *Journal of Creative Behavior* 2, no. 3 (1968).

Guessing causes

After five minutes, subjects are given the following instructions for the second task (Guessing Causes):

> In the spaces below, list as many possible causes as you can of the action shown in the picture. You may use things that might have happened just before the event in the picture or something that happened a long time ago and made the event happen. Make as many guesses as you can. Do not be afraid to guess.

Guessing consequences

After another five minutes, the following instructions are given for the third task (Guessing Consequences):

> In the spaces below, list as many possibilities as you can of what might happen as a result of what is taking place in the picture. You may use things that might happen right afterwards or things that might happen as a result long afterwards in the future. Make as many guesses as you can. Do not be afraid to guess.

The first task is designed to reveal the subject's ability to sense what he cannot find out from looking at the picture and to ask questions that will enable him to fill in the gaps in his knowledge. The second and third tasks are designed to reveal the subject's ability to formulate hypotheses concerning cause and effect. The number of relevant responses produced by a subject yields a measure of ideational fluency. The number of shifts in thinking or number of different categories of questions, causes, or consequences gives one measure of flexibility. The statistical infrequency of these questions, causes, or consequences or the extent to which the response represents a mental leap or departure from the obvious and commonplace gives one measure of originality. The detail and specificity incorporated into the questions and hypotheses provide one measure of ability to elaborate.

In another task, subjects are asked to produce unusual or provocative questions about common objects such as ice, grass, apples, or mountains. Subjects are encouraged to ask questions that lead to a variety of different answers and that might arouse interest and curiosity in others concerning the object.

Product Improvement Task

The Product Improvement Task calls for the production of clever, interesting and unusual ways of changing a toy stuffed animal (for example, a toy dog like the one in Figure 2) so that it will be more interesting and more fun for children to play with. If you would like to test yourself and see what kind of thinking is involved, try to think of ways of improving the stuffed toy dog. Limit yourself to two and one-half minutes. (In the actual test, ten minutes is allowed for this task.)

You will find a list of the commonplace or zero originality responses listed at the end of this article.

Figure 2

Unusual Uses Task

The Unusual Uses Task calls for interesting and unusual uses of common objects such as junk autos. To understand the kind of thinking that is involved, the reader might spend two and one-half minutes trying to see how many unusual uses of junk autos he can produce. At the end of the article is a list of the common, unoriginal responses that are scored zero for originality.

"Just Suppose"

The Just Suppose task presents the subject with an improbable situation and asks him to think of all of the things that might occur if that improbability really happened. In other words, the subject must "pretend" that it has happened in order to think of its possible consequences. For example, "Just suppose it was raining and all the drops stood still in the air and wouldn't move — and they were solid." Each "Just Suppose" is accompanied by an interesting drawing depicting the improbable situation. The reader might try this one, also, limiting himself to two and one-half minutes. Again, some common, unoriginal responses are listed at the end of this article.

Imaginative Stories

The Imaginative Stories Test calls for writing imaginative stories about animals and people having some divergent characteristic. Subjects are asked to select one from a set of ten titles such as:

The Flying Monkey
The Lion That Won't Roar
The Man Who Cries
The Woman Who Can but Won't Talk

Sounds and Images

The Sounds and Images Test asks the subject to produce imaginative and original images suggested by each of a series of four sound effects, ranging from a familiar and well-organized sound effect to one consisting of six rather strange and relatively unrelated sounds. The four-sound series is presented three times, and each time the subject is asked to stretch his imagination further.

Mother Goose

My newest preschool battery consists of five problems based on the world-famous Mother Goose rhymes. The four- and five-year-old children are supplied with booklets containing drawings of the five situations and encouraged to color them while they discuss the problems with the examiner. The children's booklets are used only to make the children psychologically comfortable and are retained by them. An examiner's booklet contains a set of standardized encouraging questions to be used to help the child stretch his thinking. The following is an example of a problem the reader might experiment with, using a time limit of two and one-half minutes:

If Boy Blue lost his horn, what are all of the ways that he might use to get the cows out of the corn?

Each of the tasks is based on a rationale developed from some research finding concerning the nature of the creative process, the creative personality, or the conditions necessary for creative achievement. The tasks are designed to involve as many different aspects of verbal creative functioning as possible. Most of the tasks are evaluated for fluency (number of different relevant ideas), flexibility (number of shifts in thinking or different categories of response), originality (number of statistically infrequent responses that show creative intellectual energy), and elaboration (number of different ideas used in working out the details of an idea). These are not factorially pure measures and there is some overlap among them, but it has been found that each makes a useful contribution to an understanding of a child's thinking.

Figural Battery

Although a variety of figural test tasks have been developed, the standardized batteries consist of three tasks, each designed to tap a somewhat different aspect of creative functioning.

Picture construction

The Picture Construction Test is accompanied by the following instructions:

At the bottom of this page is a piece of colored paper in the form of a curved shape. Think of a picture of an object in which this form would be an important part. Then lift up the piece of colored paper and stick it wherever you want it on the next page, just like you would a postage stamp. Then add lines with pencil or crayon to make your picture.

Try to think of a picture that no one else will think of. Keep adding new ideas to your first idea to make it tell as interesting and as exciting a story as you can.

When you have completed your picture, think up a name or title for it and write it at the bottom of the page in the space provided. Make your title as clever and unusual as possible. Use it to help tell your story.

This, as well as the other two figural tasks, can be administered at all educational levels from kindergarten to graduate school and to various occupational groups. It is a task to which kindergartners can respond in groups and one which provides sufficient encouragement to regression to be useful with graduate students and other adults. In each battery a different shape (such as a tear drop or jelly bean) is used as the stimulus object.

Figure completion

The stimulus material for the Figure Completion Test consists of ten incomplete figures and is accompanied by the following instructions:

By adding lines to figures on this and the next page, you can sketch some interesting objects or pictures. Again, try to think of some picture or object that no one else will think of. Try to make it tell as complete and as interesting a story as you can by adding to and building up your first idea. Make up a title for each of your drawings and write it at the bottom of each block next to the number of the figure.

The reader might test himself with the two figures shown in Figure 3 and then turn to the end of the article to see if he is able to get away from the common, obvious, unoriginal ideas.

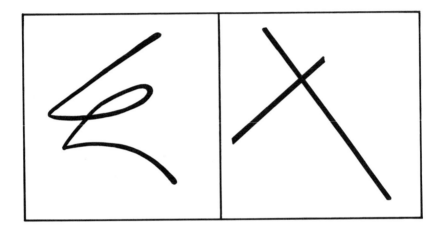

Figure 3

Repeated closed figures

The Repeated Closed Figures Test consists of two or three pages of closed figures such as triangles. The instructions for this version of the test are as follows:

In ten minutes see how many objects or pictures you can make from the triangles. . . . The triangles should be the main part of whatever you make. With pencil or crayon add lines to the triangles to complete your picture. You can place marks inside them, on them, and outside them — whatever you want to do in order to make your picture. Try to think of things that no one else will think of. Make as many different pictures or objects as you can and put as many ideas as you can in each one. Make them tell as complete and as interesting a story as you can.

As with the other two figural tests, ten minutes is allowed for this task, but in the demonstrator version only two and one-half minutes is given. The common, unoriginal responses are listed at the end of this article. . . .

110

List of common, unoriginal responses to demonstrator form (zero credit for originality)

1. *Ask Questions*

    How can it run connected only to wooden drawers?
    Why is it plugged into chest/table?
    Why is the fan blowing?
    Why is it on the chest of drawers?
    Who is he (man)?
    Is he a teacher?
    Whom is he speaking/talking to?
    What is he pointing at?
    What is he talking about?
    Why is he pointing to the fan?
    What/what kind of machine is it?
    What are the levers/buttons, etc.?
    What do the lines represent?
    What is in the drawers?

2. *Product Improvement (Toy Dog)*

    Bark, make it
    Bell, add on neck, feet, etc.
    Bow, add
    Color, add or change
    Cuddly, make it
    Ears, bigger, longer
    Eyes, bigger, move, wink, sparkle, glow, etc.
    Face, give expression, personality
    Fluffy, more like real fur
    Fuzzy, make
    Larger, longer, taller, etc.; legs longer
    Mouth, bigger
    Movable parts at joints
    Music box inside
    Noise, have him make
    Nose, bigger
    Paws, add, make bigger, etc.
    Realistic, make
    Ribbon, add brighter color, bigger bow, etc.
    Smile, make
    Softer
    Tail, curl up, make longer
    Tongue, longer

3. *Unusual Uses (Junk Autos)*

    Art, abstract, modern sculpture, pop art
    Autos, make one from several
    Autos, play on playground
    Chairs
    Demolition derby
    Demonstration, warning for drivers
    Educational uses, rebuild to learn, give to teenagers to learn about cars
    Flower planter
    Playground, pretend cars
    Racing
    Repair to sell

Scrap iron, metal, etc.
Spare parts, see for use on other cars
Swing, tires used for
Tension reducer, smash with hammer
Tires, recap and sell
Toy on playground

4. *Just Suppose (Rain Still and Solid)*

No water
No grass, no leaves on trees, no flowers, no plant life
People would be bumping into them
Earth would be parched
No fish to catch
Sunshiny, no clouds in sky
No travelling
Airplanes could not fly
Couldn't take a bath
No boating, swimming, etc.
No floods
No need for raincoats
Animals would die
No rivers, creeks, etc.

5. *Incomplete Figures*

Figure 3, left:
Abstract figure
Bird(s)
Human (man, woman, child)
Figure 3, right:
Abstract figure
Horse head or horse body
House
Kite

6. *Repeated Triangles*

Amorphous, indistinct figure
Cottage, house, etc.
Design
Human face
Human figure (man, woman, child)
Star (six-point)
Tent, tepee
Tree
Triangle

Teacher Evaluations of Creativity*

Teacher _____ Grade _____

School _____ Date _____

1. Which children in your class are the most fluent in the production of ideas? These are children who seem to be "just running over with ideas," though not always the most talkative. Some of their ideas may not be of high quality.

   1. _____
   2. _____
   3. _____
   4. _____
   5. _____

   Which are the least fluent?

   1. _____
   2. _____
   3. _____
   4. _____
   5. _____

2. Which children in your class are the most flexible in their thinking and in the production of ideas? When one plan or procedure fails, they come up immediately with a different approach. They employ a variety of strategies or approaches in solving problems. They readily abandon unproductive approaches although they do not abandon the goal: they simply find some other way of achieving the goal.

   1. _____
   2. _____
   3. _____
   4. _____
   5. _____

   Which are the least flexible?

   1. _____
   2. _____
   3. _____
   4. _____
   5. _____

---

* Reproduced from *Torrance Tests of Creative Thinking, Norms—Technical Manual* by E. Paul Torrance (Lexington, Mass.: Personnel Press, 1974).

3. Which children in your class are the most original in their thinking? They are able to get away from the obvious and the commonplace and break away from the beaten path. They see relationships and think of ideas and solutions which are different from others in the class and from the textbook. Many, though not all, of their ideas prove to be useful. Some of their ideas are quite surprising, though true.

1. _____
2. _____
3. _____
4. _____
5. _____

Which are the least original?

1. _____
2. _____
3. _____
4. _____
5. _____

4. Which children in your class are the best in elaborating ideas? They are able to take an idea or a task and spell out the detail. They can take a simple idea and "embroider" it or make it fancy and attractive. Their drawings are very detailed and they are able to develop very detailed or thorough plans for projects.

1. _____
2. _____
3. _____
4. _____
5. _____

Which are least able to elaborate?

1. _____
2. _____
3. _____
4. _____
5. _____

Sources of Instruments

A List of Representative Tests for the Six U.S.O.E. Talent Areas*

U.S.O.E. Talent Area Area I: General Intellectual Ability

Title of Instrument	Age Range	Scores	Time	Publisher [1]	MMY or TIP [2] Ref.
INDIVIDUAL TESTS					
Peabody Picture Vocabulary Test (PPVT)	2½-18 years	Mental Age, Deviation I.Q.	10-15 min.	American Guidance Service	7:417
Progressive Matrices (Raven)	5 years and over	Percentiles	60 min.	Psychological Corporation	7:376
Slosson Intelligence Test (SIT)	2 weeks and over	Mental Age, I.Q.	30 min.	Slosson Educational Publications Dublin, N.H. 03444	7:424
Stanford Binet Intelligence Scale	2-18 years	Mental Age, I.Q.	30-90 min.	Houghton-Mifflin Company	7:425
Wechsler Adult Intelligence Scale (WAIS)	16-64 years	Verbal I.Q. Performance I.Q. Full Scale I.Q.	60-90 min.	Psychological Corporation	7:429
Wechsler Intelligence Scale for Children—Revised (WISC)	6-16 years	Verbal I.Q. Performance I.Q. Full Scale I.Q.	60-90 min.	Psychological Corporation	7:431
Wechsler Primary and Preschool Scale of Intelligence (WPPSI)	4-6½ years	Verbal I.Q. Performance I.Q. Full Scale I.Q.	60-90 min.	Psychological Corporation	7:434

[1] A list of the test publishers follows.
[2] MMY reference is the **Mental Measurements Yearbooks** volume and entry number for the latest review of the test listed. TIP refers to **Tests in Print II**. It is recommended that MMY and TIP citations be reviewed before an instrument is used.

*From "Identification and Evaluation Procedures for Gifted and Talented Programs" by Ron Rubenzer, **Gifted Child Quarterly** 23, no. 2 (Summer 1979) 313–16.

Title of Instrument	Age Range	Scores	Time	Publisher	MMY or TIP Ref.
GROUP TESTS					
California Tests of Mental Maturity 1963 Revision (CTMM)	4-16	Standard Scores	90 min.	California Test Bureau	7:338
Lorge-Thorndike Intelligence Tests	K-12	Verbal and Nonverbal Deviation I.Q. Age, grade, percentiles	K-3rd = 35 min. 4-12th = 90 min.	Houghton-Mifflin Company	7:360
Otis-Lennon Mental Ability Test	K-16	Deviation I.Q. Percentiles & Stanines	30 min.	Harcourt, Brace & World	7:370
Short Form of Academic Aptitude	1.5-12	Verbal and Nonverbal Total	30-45 min.	CTB/McGraw-Hill Book Co. 330 W. 42nd St. New York, N.Y. 10036	7:387

U.S.O.E. Area II: Specific Academic Aptitude

Title of Instrument	Age Range	Scores	Time	Publisher	MMY or TIP Ref.
INDIVIDUAL TESTS Gates-MacGinitie Reading Tests	K-12	Vocabulary-comprehension	120 min. (8 subtests)	Teachers College Press	7:689
Key Math Tests	K-7	15 scores involving content, operations, applications	30 min.	American Guidance Service	721 TIP
Metropolitan Readiness Tests	K-1	7 or 8 scores	75 min.	Harcourt, Brace & World	7:757
Peabody Individual Achievement Test (PIAT)	K-12	6 scores—math, reading comp., spelling, gen. info. total	30-40 min.	American Guidance Service	7:17

Title of Instrument	Age Range	Scores	Time	Publisher	MMY or TIP Ref.
Woodcock Reading Mastery Test	K-12	6 scores—letter and word ident., word attach, word comp., passage comp. total	45 min.	American Guidance Service	1656 (TIP)
GROUP TESTS					
Iowa Tests of Basic Skills	3-9	Grade Equivs., Percentiles and others	279 min. (4 sessions)	Science Research Associates	6:13
Metropolitan Achievement Test	1-12	Grade Equivs., Percentiles and others	227-316 min. (in sessions)	Harcourt, Brace & World	7:14
Sequential Tests of Educational Progress (STEP)	4-14	Grade Equivs., Percentiles and others	240 min. (3 sessions)	Educational Testing Service (Cooperative Test Division)	6:25
Stanford Achievement Test	1-12	Grade Equivs., Percentiles and others	303 min. (in sessions)	Harcourt, Brace & World	7:25
TEACHER SCREENING DEVICES					
Cupertino School District, Extended Learning Program: Screening and Nomination Form	K-12	Weighted scores in cognitive & non-cognitive areas.	Not indicated.	Programs for Gifted Students Educational Improvement Center Woodbury Glassboro Road—Box 426 Pitman, N.J. 08071	

117

Title of Instrument	Age Range	Scores	Time	Publisher	MMY or TIP Ref.
Multi-Dimensional Screening Device (MDSD)	2-7	Numerical rating in 10 talent areas. Appropriate for Disadvantaged.	2-3 hrs. whole class	Hella Kranz Fairfax County Public Schools 10700 Page Ave. Fairfax, Va. 22030	
Reservoir Model for Identification of the Gifted and Talented	K-12	A general screening process.	Not indicated.	Gowan, J. C. "How to Identify Students for a Gifted Child Program," **Gifted Child Quarterly, XIX,** (3), 1975, 260-263.	
Scales for Rating the Behavioral Characteristics of Superior Students	K-12	Numerical rating in 10 talent areas.	Not indicated.	Joseph Renzulli Creative Learning Press P.O. Box 320 Mansfield Center, Ct. 06250	
U.S.O.E. Area III: Creative or Productive Thinking					
INDIVIDUAL TESTS Creativity Tests for Children (CTC)	4-6	10 tests—measures Guilford's divergent production abilities.		Sheridan Psychological Services	554 (TIP)
Remote Associates Test (RAT)	9-16, and adults	Measures ability to think creatively	40-45 min.	Houghton-Mifflin Co.	7:445
Torrance Tests of Creative Thinking	K-Grad. School	Verbal & Pictorial scores in fluency, flexibility, originality, & elaboration	Verbal— 60 min. Nonverbal— 45 min. (can be given without time constraints)	Personnel Press 191 Spring St. Lexington, Mass. 02173	7:448

Title of Instrument	Age Range	Scores	Time	Publisher	MMY or TIP Ref.
GROUP TESTS					
Alpha-Biographical Inventory	9-12	Creativity; Academic performance in College.	90-120 min.	Prediction Press P.O. Box 298 Greensboro, N.C. 27402	7:975
The Adjective Check List	9-16, and adults	24 scores related to creativity	15-20 min.	Consulting Psycho-logists Press, Inc.	7:38

U.S.O.E. Area IV: Leadership Ability

Title of Instrument	Age Range	Scores	Time	Publisher	MMY or TIP Ref.
INDIVIDUAL TESTS					
Personal Interview Techniques	9-12			Research and Guidance Laboratory University of Wisconsin Madison, Wisconsin Educational Science I Bldg. 1025 W. Johnson Street Madison, Wisconsin	
GROUP TESTS					
Leadership scale of the Multi-dimensional Screening Device	REFER TO SPECIFIC ACADEMIC APTITUDE SECTION.				
Leadership scale of the Scales for Rating the Behavioral Characteristics of Superior Students	REFER TO SPECIFIC ACADEMIC APTITUDE SECTION.				

U.S.O.E. Area V: Visual and Performing Arts

Title of Instrument	Age Range	Scores	Time	Publisher	MMY or TIP Ref.
INDIVIDUAL TESTS					
Music: Seashore Measure of Musical Talents, Revised Edition	4-16	6 scores—pitch, loudness, rhythm, time, timbre, tonal measure	60 min.	Psychological Corp.	6:353
Art: Horn Art Aptitude Inventory	12-16, and adults	Scribbling and doodling, and imagery.	50 min.	Horn-Stoelting Co. 1350 South Kostner Avenue Chicago, Ill. 60623	5:242
Meier Art Tests	7-16, and adults	Percentile Norms for Art Judgment Aesthetic Perception	60 min.	Bureau of Educational Research and Service University of Iowa Iowa City, Iowa 25240	7:240

U.S.O.E. Area VI: Psychomotor Ability

INDIVIDUAL TEST	REFER TO GENERAL INTELLECTUAL ABILITY (INDIVIDUAL TESTS)				
Performance Scale I.Q.'s of the Wechsler Series					
GROUP TESTS					
Guilford Zimmerman Aptitude Survey	9-16, and adults	7 aptitude areas investigated	163 min. (7 tests)	Sheridan Psychological Services	6:772
Differential Aptitude Tests	8-12	Stanines and Percentiles	240 min. (2–6 sess.)	Psychological Corp.	7:673

American Guidance Service, Inc., Publishers' Building, Circle Pines, Minn. 55014.
California Test Bureau, Del Monte Research Park, Monterey, Calif. 93940.
Educational Testing Service, Princeton, N.J. 08540.
Harcourt, Brace & World, Inc., 757 Third Avenue, New York, N.Y. 10017.
Houghton Mifflin Company, 110 Tremont Street, Boston, Mass. 02107.
Psychological Corporation, 304 East 45th Street, New York, N.Y. 10017.
Science Research Associates, Inc., 259 East Erie Street, Chicago, Ill. 60611.
Sheridan Psychological Services, P.O., Box 837, Beverly Hills, Calif. 90213.
Teachers College Press, Teachers College, 525 West 120th Street, New York, N.Y. 10027.

MMY and TIP references can be located in the following publications:

Buros, O.K. (Ed.) *Tests in Print II*, Highland Park, New Jersey, The Gryphon Press, 1974.

Buros, O.K. (Ed.) *The Seventh Mental Measurements Yearbook*, Highland Park, New Jersey, The Gryphon Press, 1972.

Buros, O.K. (Ed.) *The Sixth Mental Measurements Yearbook*, Highland Park, New Jersey, The Gryphon Press, 1972.

Buros, O.K. (Ed.) *The Fourth Mental Measurements Yearbook*, Highland Park, New Jersey, The Gryphon Press, 1972.

Tests for Assessing Higher-Level Thinking Behavior

TEST	AUTHOR	VARIABLE TESTED	SOURCE	AGE
1. Butch and Slim, Test of Propositional Logic	J. Ward	Analysis (Propositional Logic)	J. Ward, "The Saga of Butch and Slim," **British Journal of Educational Psychology** 42:267–289, 1972	8–adolescent
2. Classification Tasks	Mary Nixon	Analysis	Senior Advisory Officer Psychological Services, Australian Council for Educational Research, P.O. Box 219, Hawthorn, Victoria, Australia 3122	4–8 years
3. Cornell Class, Reasoning Test, Form X	Robert H. Ennis William L. Gardiner Richard Morrow Dieter Paulus Lucille Ringel	Evaluation (class reasoning)	Illinois Critical Thinking Project, 371 Education Building, University of Urbana-Champaign, Urbana, Illinois 61801	10–18 years
4. Cornell Conditional Reasoning Test, Form X		Evaluation (class reasoning)	Illinois Critical Thinking Project, 371 Education Building, University of Illinois at Urbana-Champaign, Urbana, Illinois 61801	10–18 years
5. Inquiry Skill	Daniel Solomon Arthur Kendall	Synthesis (developing a strategy)	Daniel Solomon, Psychological Services Section, Montgomery County Public Schools, 850 Hungerford Drive, Rockville, Maryland 20850	9–15 years

* Adapted from a list compiled by Donald Nasca, 1978.

TEST	AUTHOR	VARIABLE TESTED	SOURCE	AGE
6. Literature Formal Reasoning Test	William M. Bart	Analysis (formal reasoning)	William M. Bart, Department of Psychological Foundations, College of Education, 330 Burton Hall, University of Minnesota, Minneapolis, Minnesota 55455	14 and up
7. Means-Ends Problem-Solving (MEPS)	Jerome J. Platt George Spivack	Synthesis	Division of Research and Evaluation, Department of Mental Health Sciences, Hahnemann Medical College and Hospital, 314 North Broad Street, Philadelphia, Pennsylvania 19102	6–adult
8. Object Sorting Task (OST)	James A. Dunn	Synthesis (fluency)	The OST: Theory, Instrument and Norms, James A. Dunn, American Institute for Research, P.O. Box 1113, Palo Alto, California 94302	5 and up
9. Ordering Tasks	Barbara Brandes Susan Rindler	Analysis	Research for Better Schools, Inc., Public Information Office, 1700 Market Street, Philadelphia, Pennsylvania 19103	10–14 years
10. Paulus Conditional Reasoning Test, Form Z (assessing)	Dieter Paulus	Evaluation (conditional reasoning)	Dieter H. Paulus, U-64, Department of Educational Psychology, University of Connecticut, Storrs, Connecticut 06268	12–16 years

123

TEST	AUTHOR	VARIABLE TESTED	SOURCE	AGE
11. Pictorial Class Inclusion Problems	Giyoo Hatano Keiko Kuhara	Analysis (class inclusion)	A complete manual of the test can be obtained from Giyoo Hatano, 7-12 Honkomgome-6, Bunkyo-ku, Tokyo, 113, Japan (no charge)	5–7 years
12. Purdue Elementary Problem Solving Inventory	John Feldhusen John Houtz Susan Ringenbach	Multiple (Analysis, Synthesis, and Evaluation	John Feldhusen, Educational Psychology and Research Section, Purdue University, SCC-G Lafayette, Indiana 47907	5–11 years
13. Ross Test of Higher Cognitive Processes	John D. Ross Catherine Ross	Analysis	Academic Therapy Publications, P.O. Box 899, 1539 4th Street, San Rafael, California 94901	Intermediate
14. The Tests of Pre-Literature Thinking Aptitude	Rachel S. Ball	Multiple (Analysis and Synthesis)	"A Longitudinal Assessment of Thinking Ability of Preliterate Children During a 2-Yr. Period," Rachel Ball, Arizona State University, Tempe, Arizona 85281	3–5 years
15. Khatena-Torrance Creative Perception Inventory	Khatena and Torrance	Affective	Manual for Khatena-Torrance Creative Perception Inventory, Stoeltling Company, 1350 South Kostner Avenue, Chicago, Illinois 60623	Adolescent and up
16. Scale of Academic Curiosity	Derek C. Vidler Hashim R. Rawan	Affective	Derek Vidler, Box 1661, Hunter College of City University of New York, New York, New York 10021	8 and up

TEST	AUTHOR	VARIABLE TESTED	SOURCE	AGE
17. Ascher-Gallagher System	Mary Jane Ascher and others	Cognitive	Mary J. Ascher, et al., "A System for Classifying Thought Processes in the Context of Classroom Verbal Interaction," Institute for Research on Exceptional Children, University of Illinois, Urbana, Illinois	Any classroom
18. Cognitive Levels Analysis Interaction Model	Kenneth Shrable Douglas Minnis	Cognitive	Kenneth Shrable and Douglas Minnis, "Interacting in the Interrogative," **Journal of Teacher Education** 21: 201–12, 1969	Any classroom
19. Florida Taxonomy of Cognitive Behaviors	Bob Burton Brown and others	Cognitive	Brown, Bob Burton, et al., "The Florida Taxonomy of Cognitive Behaviors: Directions," University of Florida, Gainesville, 1967	Any classroom
20. Taba System	Hilda Taba and others	Cognitive, Affective, and Procedural		Any classroom
21. Waimon System	Morton D. Waimon	Cognitive, Affective, and Procedural	Morton D. Waimon and Henry J. Hermanzwicz, "Helping Prospective Teachers Classify and Study Teaching Behavior," **Teachers College Journal** 38: 97–102, 1966	Any classroom

Selected References

Books and Articles

Abraham, W. *Common Sense About Gifted Children.* New York: Harper and Bros., 1958.

Anastasi, Anne. *Psychological Testing.* 4th ed. New York: Macmillan, 1976.

Assagioli, Roberto. "The Education of Gifted and Super-Gifted Children." New York: Psychosynthesis Foundation, 1960.

Biondi, A. and Parnes, S. *Assessing Creative Growth.* Vol. 1 and 2. Great Neck, N.Y.: Creative Synergetic Association, 1976.

Boston, Bruce O. *A Resource Manual of Information on Educating the Gifted and Talented.* Reston, Va.: Council for Exceptional Children, 1975.

Buros, Oscar K., ed. *Tests in Print II.* Highland Park, N.J.: Gryphon Press, 1974.

──────. *Mental Measurements Yearbook.* Highland Park, N.J.: Gryphon Press, 1978.

Clark, Barbara. *Growing Up Gifted.* Columbus, Ohio: Charles E. Merrill Publishing Co., 1979.

Comrey, Andrew; Backer, Thomas; and Glaser, Edward. *A Sourcebook for Mental Health Measures.* Human Interaction Institute, 10889 Wilshire Blvd., Los Angeles, Calif. 90024.

Deakin, Michael. *The Children on the Hill.* London: Quartet Books, 1972.

DeHaan, R., and Havighurst, R. J. *Educating Gifted Children.* Chicago: University of Chicago Press, 1957.

Fortna, Richard O., and Boston, Bruce O. *Testing the Gifted Child: An Interpretation in Lay Language.* Reston, Va.: Council for Exceptional Children, 1976.

Gallagher, J. J. *Teaching the Gifted Child.* Boston: Allyn and Bacon, 1975.

──────. *Research Summary on Gifted Child Education.* Springfield, Ill.: Office of the Superintendent of Public Instruction, 1966.

Gold, Milton. *Education of the Intellectually Gifted.* Columbus, Ohio: Charles E. Merrill, 1965.

Gowan, J.; Khatena, J.; and Torrance, E. P., eds. *Educating the Ablest.* Itasca, Ill.: F. E. Peacock Publishing, Inc., 1979.

Johnson, Orval G. *Tests and Measurement in Child Development: Handbook II.* Vol. 1 and 2. San Francisco: Jossey-Bass, 1976.

Kerlinger, Fred N. *Foundations of Behavioral Research.* New York: Holt, Rinehart, and Winston, 1973.

Lyon, H. "Education of the Gifted and Talented." *Exceptional Children* 43, no. 3 (1976) : 166–67.

Macrorie, Ken. "A Room with Class." *Media and Methods* 14, no. 5, January 1978.

Martinson, R. A. "Research on the Gifted and Talented: Its Implication for Education." In *Education of the Gifted and Talented: Report to the Congress of the United States by the U.S. Commissioner of Education.* Washington, D.C.: Government Printing Office, 1972.

————, and Seagoe, May V. *The Abilities of Young Children.* Reston, Va.: Council for Exceptional Children, 1967.

————. *The Identification of the Gifted and Talented.* Ventura, Calif.: Ventura County Superintendent of Schools, 1974.

Nolte, Jane. "Nearly . . . Everything You've Always Wanted to Know About the Gifted and Talented." Wauwatosa, Wisconsin Council for the Gifted and Talented, 1976.

Pearce, Joseph C. *Magical Child.* New York: Dutton, 1977.

Star Power: Providing for the Gifted and Talented. Instructional Services, Region XIII Education Service Center, 7703 North Lamar, Austin, Texas 78752.

Torrance, E. Paul. *Discovery and Nurturance of Giftedness in the Culturally Different.* Reston, Va.: Council for Exceptional Children, 1977.

Treffinger, Donald, J., and Curl, Clifford D. *Self-Directed Study Guide on the Education of the Gifted and Talented.* Ventura, Calif.: Ventura County Superintendent of Schools, 1976.

Tuttle, Frederick B., Jr. *Gifted and Talented Students.* Washington, D.C.: National Education Association, 1978.

Periodicals

G/C/T
Box 66654
Mobile, AL 36606

Gifted Child Quarterly
National Association for Gifted Children
217 Gregory Drive
Hot Springs, AR 71901

Exceptional Children
Council for Exceptional Children
1920 Association Drive
Reston, VA 22091

National/State Leadership Training Institute on the Gifted and
Talented *Bulletin*
Civic Center Tower Building
316 West Second Street, Suite PH-C
Los Angeles, CA 90012

Education Unlimited
1834 Meetinghouse Road
Boothwyn, PA 19061

Dromenon
Box 2244
New York, NY 10011

Media

Sit Down, Shut Up, or Get Out (film)
Broadcasting and Film Commission
c/o National Council of Churches
475 Riverside Drive
New York, NY 10027

Understanding the Gifted (film)
Churchill Films
662 North Robertson Boulevard
Los Angeles, CA 90069

More Than a Glance (film)
Who Is the Gifted Child? (filmstrip)
Audiovisual Services
Ventura County Superintendent of Schools
County Office Building
535 East Main Street
Ventura, CA 93001

Art and Multi-Sensory Experience (filmstrip series)
Educational Frontiers Associates
Avenel, NJ 07001

Who Are These People? (film)
Scott Anderson Productions
Reston, VA 22091

Simple Gifts (videotapes)
University of Wisconsin Telecommunications Center
WHA-TV
Madison, WI 53706

Threat or Invitation:
  Characteristics of Gifted and Talented
  Identification of Gifted and Talented
      (videotapes by Frederick B. Tuttle, Jr., and Laurence A. Becker)
Educational Communications Center
State University of New York, College at Brockport
Brockport, NY 14420

Talks with Teachers About Gifted and Talented Students:
  Characteristics
  Identification
  Parents of the Gifted and Talented: A Teacher's View
  A Parent's View of Gifted and Talented Children
      (audiotapes)
National Education Association
1201 16th Street, NW
Washington, DC 20036

ACTIVITIES FOR TEACHERS

1. RIPPLES

We are all prospectors—searching for rare gems. Months of digging, scratching, clawing, sweating may uncover one—but what a one!

When I want him to call on me, I look sleepy.

(A student's strategy)

I'm Me

I'm me,
That's all I can be.
Not stamped out of cookie cutter,
But like a silver blossom made to flutter.
Plain and simple me.
I can't help it,
I'm me,
Who else can I be?
(Lillian M., quoted in "Recent Insights on the Culturally Different Gifted" by Catherine B. Bruch and J. A. Curry, *Gifted Child Quarterly* 22: 374–93; Fall 1978.)

Birthday Poem for a Student-Turned-Colleague

Pursuing chimeras of apathy,
Bearing the brunt of tensions not your own,
A restless leader impatient with ennui,
You once in middy stood: a girl half-grown.
Then, inchoate dreams and netted thoughts
Struggled toward a metamorphosis
Into bright wings of fancy. And painfully-wrought,
You poured your soul into such urns as this.
I saw each urn take form, the butterflies
Take flight, and had a privilege only those
Who teach may feel—to watch with pleased surprise
A budding talent bloom into a rose:
    My birthday gift for you, had I the power,
    Would be you'd have, as teacher, one such flower.
(Joan Mellard, *English Journal* 67, no. 5; May 1978).

Add your thought and comments.

2. EXAMINATION OF INSTRUMENTS

In the space following each type of instrument or method, list the administration requirements, what is measured, advantages, and limitations. The example illustrates the activity.

Group IQ Tests

> *Instrument Examined:* California Tests of Mental Measurement
>
> *Administration Requirements:* Untrained supervisor of testing situation, individual or machine scoring, exact reading of directions, no extra help or prodding.
>
> *What Is Measured:* General aptitude or learning potential.
>
> *Advantages:* Ease of administration to large groups, less expensive than individual tests, consistency of scoring.
>
> *Limitations:* Students cannot explain their reasons of answers given, lines of reasoning cannot be pursued, congruent thinking seems to be favored and divergent thinking penalized ...

Instrument Examined: _____

_____

_____

Administration Requirements: _____

_____

_____

What Is Measured: _____

_____

_____

Advantages: _____

_____

_____

Limitations: _____

_____

_____

Notes: _____

_____

_____

Achievement Tests

    Instrument Examined: _____

_____

_____

    Administration Requirements: _____

_____

_____

    What Is Measured: _____

_____

_____

    Advantages: _____

_____

_____

    Limitations: _____

_____

_____

    Notes: _____

_____

_____

Individualized IQ Tests

    Instrument Examined: _____

_____

_____

    Administration Requirements: _____

_____

_____

    What Is Measured: _____

_____

_____

Advantages: _____

_____

_____

Limitations: _____

_____

_____

Notes: _____

_____

_____

Behavioral Checklists

Instrument Examined: _____

_____

_____

Administration Requirements: _____

_____

_____

What Is Measured: _____

_____

_____

Advantages: _____

_____

_____

Limitations: _____

_____

_____

Notes: _____

_____

_____

Biographical Inventories

Instrument Examined : _____

_____

_____

Administration Requirements : _____

_____

_____

What Is Measured : _____

_____

_____

Advantages : _____

_____

_____

Limitations : _____

_____

_____

Notes : _____

_____

_____

Teacher Nominations

Instrument Examined : _____

_____

_____

Administration Requirements : _____

_____

_____

What Is Measured : _____

_____

_____

Advantages: _____

_____

_____

Limitations: _____

_____

_____

Notes: _____

_____

_____

Creativity Tests

Instrument Examined: _____

_____

_____

Administration Requirements: _____

_____

_____

What Is Measured: _____

_____

_____

Advantages: _____

_____

_____

Limitations: _____

_____

_____

Notes: _____

_____

_____

Culture Fair Tests

Instrument Examined: _____

_____

_____

Administration Requirements: _____

_____

_____

What Is Measured: _____

_____

_____

Advantages: _____

_____

_____

Limitations: _____

_____

_____

Notes: _____

_____

_____

Transcripts

Instrument Examined: _____

_____

_____

Administration Requirements: _____

_____

_____

What Is Measured: _____

_____

_____

Advantages: _____

_____

_____

Limitations: _____

_____

_____

Notes: _____

_____

_____

Parent Nominations

Instrument Examined: _____

_____

_____

Administration Requirements: _____

_____

_____

What Is Measured: _____

_____

_____

Advantages: _____

_____

_____

Limitations: _____

_____

_____

Notes: _____

_____

_____

Peer Nominations

Instrument Examined: _____

_____

_____

Administration Requirements: _____

_____

_____

What Is Measured: _____

_____

_____

Advantages: _____

_____

_____

Limitations: _____

_____

_____

Notes: _____

_____

_____

Self-Nominations

Instrument Examined: _____

_____

_____

Administration Requirements: _____

_____

_____

What Is Measured: _____

_____

_____

Advantages: _____

_____

_____

Limitations: _____

_____

_____

Notes: _____

_____

_____

3. SELECTION OF INSTRUMENTS AND METHODS

After surveying several samples of instruments and methods in each area, you should be ready to select those which you believe will best identify students for your particular program. These instruments should help identify the characteristics most pertinent to your program and curriculum. Using those characteristics you believe to be most important (see Supplementary Materials, Lists of Characteristics), list the instruments you would use to identify students for your program.

In the spaces given fill in the information for the specific instruments or device selected.

Objective Instruments (e.g., group IQ, achievement)

Specific Test: _____

_____

Pertinent Characteristics Identified: _____

_____

Notes: _____

_____

Specific Test: _____

_____

Pertinent Characteristics Identified: _____

_____

Notes: _____

_____

Individual Methods (e.g., individual IQ, biographical inventory, behavioral checklist)

Specific Test: _____

_____

Pertinent Characteristics Identified: _____

_____

Notes: _____

_____

Specific Test: _____

_____

Pertinent Characteristics Identified: _____

_____

Notes: _____

_____

Specific Test: _____

_____

Pertinent Characteristics Identified: _____

_____

Notes: _____

_____

Specific Test: _____

_____

Pertinent Characteristics Identified: _____

_____

Notes: _____

_____

Other Methods (grades, teacher nominations, student nominations)

Specific Test: _____

_____

Pertinent Characteristics Identified: _____

_____

Notes: _____

_____

Specific Test: _____

_____

Pertinent Characteristics Identified: _____

_____

Notes: _____

_____

Specific Test: _____

_____

Pertinent Characteristics Identified: _____

_____

Notes: _____

_____

Specific Test: _____

_____

Pertinent Characteristics Identified: _____

_____

Notes: _____

_____

Specific Test: _____

_____

Pertinent Characteristics Identified: _____

_____

Notes: _____

_____

Acknowledgments *(Continued)*

Programs for the Gifted Rating Scales for Kindergarten Students and First Grade Students; Rating Scales #1–4 (Grades 2–6 only); and Teacher Recommendation Checklist — Junior High (revised 1977), prepared by Department of Exceptional Child Education, Dade County (Florida) Public Schools. Checklist for Recommending Gifted and Creative Students (Middle Grades and Above), by William B. Cummings, San Francisco Unified School District Programs for Mentally Gifted Minors. "Checklist for the Identification of Culturally Disadvantaged Underachieving Mentally Gifted Minors" by Paul Plowman, California State Department of Education, Sacramento, 1968. "Characteristics of Able Disadvantaged Pupils" from Los Angeles Unified School District. Self-Portrait, Autobiographical Questionnaire, Recommendation Form, and Student Application Form from Horizons Unlimited, Keene State College, Keene, New Hampshire. Sample items from *Biographical Inventory: Form U*, Institute for Behavioral Research in Creativity (IBRIC), Salt Lake City, Utah, 1976. Parent Questionnaire, including Examiner Instructions, by Margot Nicholas Parrot as part of a grant awarded to the Bucksport/Orland Gifted Task Force by the Maine Department of Educational and Cultural Services from funding obtained from the U.S. Office of Gifted and Talented, Washington, D.C., June 1978. Peer Referral Form and Teacher-Community Member Referral Form from Project Discovery, Oak Hill High School, Wales, Maine. Peer Identification-Creativity Forms: Elementary and Secondary by John Ferrell, Director, and Glenn Poshard, Consultant, Franklin County Region 7 Area Service Center for Educators of Gifted Children, Marion, Illinois. Talent Survey Form from the Delphi Program, Greece Central School District, Greece, New York. Excerpt from "Examples and Rationales of Test Tasks for Assessing Creative Abilities" by E. Paul Torrance, from *Journal of Creative Behavior* 2, no. 3 (1968); copyright © 1968 by the Creative Education Foundation, Inc. "Teacher Evaluations of Creativity" from *Torrance Tests of Creative Thinking, Norms-Technical Manual* by E. Paul Torrance; copyright © 1974 by Personnel Press, Lexington, Massachusetts. "A List of Representative Tests for the Six U.S.O.E. Talent Areas" from "Identification and Evaluation Procedures for Gifted and Talented Programs" by Ron Rubenzer; © 1979 by National Association for Gifted Children; reprinted by permission from the *Gifted Child Quarterly* 23, no. 2 (Summer 1979), pp. 313–16. "Tests for Assessing Higher-Level Thinking Behavior" adapted from list compiled by Donald Nasca, Bureau of Educational Field Services, State University of New York, College at Brockport, 1978. "I'm Me" by Lillian M., quoted in "Recent Insights on the Culturally Different Gifted" by Catherine B. Bruch and J. A. Curry in *Gifted Child Quarterly*, Fall 1978; copyright © 1978 by National Association for Gifted Children. "Birthday Poem for a Student-Turned-Colleague" by Joan Mellard in *English Journal*, May 1978; copyright © 1978 by the National Council of Teachers of English.

SONIC SELECT
BOOK FOUR

W9-CCA-107

writers
DAN SLOTT, MIKE GALLAGHER,
KARL BOLLERS, KEN PENDERS,
EVAN SKOLNICK, JIM SPIVEY,
& FRANK STROM

artists
JIM VALENTINO, PATRICK "SPAZ" SPAZIANTE,
JAMES FRY, BOB WIACEK, JOSH RAY, AIMEE RAY,
FRANK STROM, JIM AMASH, ANDREW PEPOY,
BARRY GROSSMAN, HARVEY MERCADDOCASIO,
SUZANNE PADDOCK, JEFF POWELL, VICKIE WILLIAMS,
RICH KOSLOWSKI & ART MAWHINNEY

cover by
PATRICK "SPAZ" SPAZIANTE

SPECIAL THANKS TO CINDY CHAU @ SEGA LICENSING

ARCHIE COMIC PUBLICATIONS, INC.
JONATHAN GOLDWATER, co-ceo
NANCY SILBERKLEIT, co-ceo
MIKE PELLERITO, president
VICTOR GORELICK, co-president/editor-in-chief
BILL HORAN, director of circulation
HAROLD BUCHHOLZ, executive director of
publishing/operations
ALEX SEGURA, executive director of
publicity & marketing
PAUL KAMINSKI, compilation editor
STEPHEN OSWALD, production manager
IAN FLYNN, compilation consultant
JAMIE LEE ROTANTE, proofreader
JON GRAY, SUZANNAH ROWNTREE
& VIN LOVALLO, production

TABLE OF CONTENTS

"Turnabout Heroes" (Sonic Super Special #12):
Why does Knuckles look like he's ready to
run at Mach 10? Why is Sonic rad, red and ready
to guard the floating island?! It's a freaky Friday
indeed when Dr. Robotnik and Dimitri team up to
defeat our heroes! Will the Freedom Fighters
and the Chaotix be able to help their
respective leaders in time?

"Den of Thieves" (Sonic Super Special #8):
Monkey Khan is bringin' the ruckus to
the Dragon Kingdom! But not even the help
of Lau Fang will be able to save everyone's
favorite super-simian from an army of
deadly Yagyu ninjas!

"Law of the Land" (Sonic Super Special #14):
When a mysterious Zone Portal opens up
in the forest, Sonic is transported away to one
twisted town! One where the evil Robotnik
Enterprises is the judge, jury and executioner
of all who reside within! Help!

"Sonic Blast" (Sonic Blast):
Adventure abounds on Flickie Island!
It's Sonic vs Robotnik for the fate of the Flickies
in this classic Sega game-adaptation!

SONIC SUPER SPECIAL

THE PLANET MOBIUS WAS ONCE A VIRTUAL PARADISE UNTIL IT WAS CONQUERED BY THE EVIL DOCTOR ROBOTNIK! HIS TECHNOLOGICAL TYRANNY WOULD HAVE CONTINUED IF NOT FOR A HEROIC GROUP OF FREEDOM FIGHTERS WHO BANDED TOGETHER AND RESTORED ORDER TO THE KINGDOM OF ACORN! THE BRAVEST AMONG THEM IS A BLUE STREAK FILLED WITH THE MOST ATTITUDE GOING AROUND — AND, WITHOUT A DOUBT, HE IS THE MOST FASTEST THING ALIVE!
ARCHIE COMICS AND SEGA PRESENT... SONIC THE HEDGEHOG!

ZONE WARS: PRELUDE

Dan Slott — Writer
James Fry — Penciler
Bob Wiacek — Inker
Jeff Powell — Letterer
Josh D. Ray — Colors
& Interior Separations

J.F. Gabrie — Editor

Victor Gorelick — Managing Editor
Richard Goldwater — Editor-In-Chief

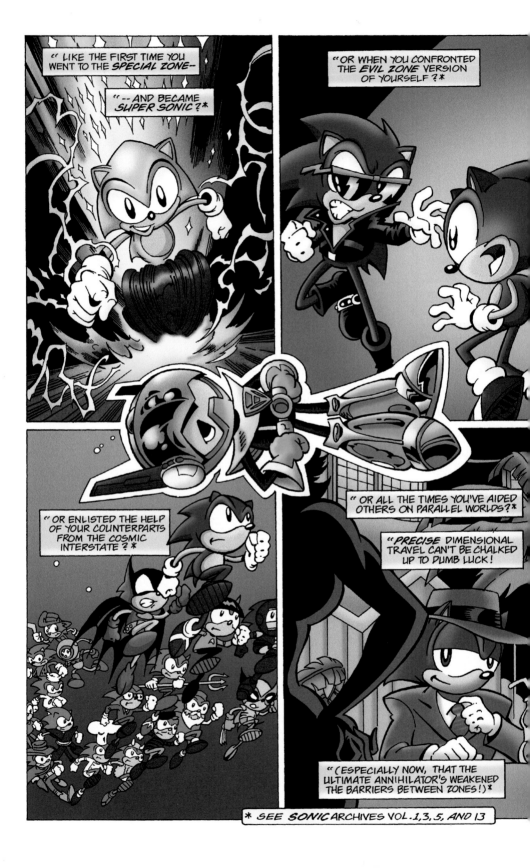

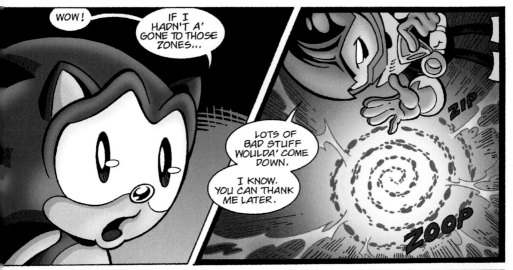

AND ON THAT SOUR NOTE...

⧽SIGH⧽

I'D BETTER HAVE MY SWEEP-BOTS CLEAN UP THAT AWFUL HEDGEHOG'S LITTER...

...BEFORE HE AND HIS FREEDOM FIGHTING FRIENDS TURN THE GREAT FOREST INTO A GIANT GARBAGE DUMP...

"...THE SAME AS THEY DID TO MOBOTROPOLIS!"

KINTOBOR MADE US LOOK LIKE COMPLETE IDIOTS...

...AGAIN! SONIC--YOU USED TO BE SUCH A GO-GETTER!

WHAT HAPPENED TO THE HEDGEHOG WHO HELPED ME TOSS MY DAD INTO THE ZONE OF SILENCE?

HE EEZ OFF SOMEWHERE POWDEREENG HIS NOSE, PERHAPS?

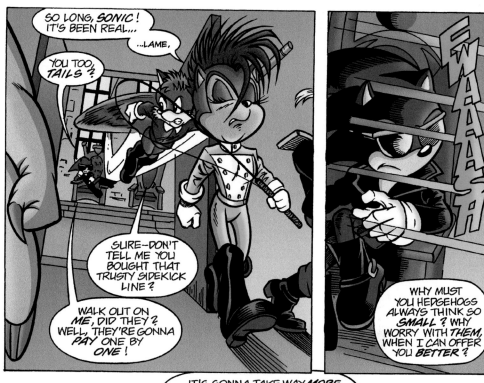

YOU AGAIN?

YES, SONIC--I NEED YOUR *HELP*, IMMEDIATELY!

MY HELP?

SONIC-- WHO IS HE?

I'M A *ZONE COP*-- MY DUTY IS TO MAKE SURE NO ONE *STRAYS* FROM THEIR OWN ZONE.

WE'RE RIGHT WHERE WE OUGHTTA BE! SO, WHY'D YOU *CRASH* OUR PICNIC, SUGAH-SHERIFF?

BECAUSE ONLY *HE* CAN HELP STOP THIS *NEW MENACE*!

WELL, *WHERE* DO WE START?

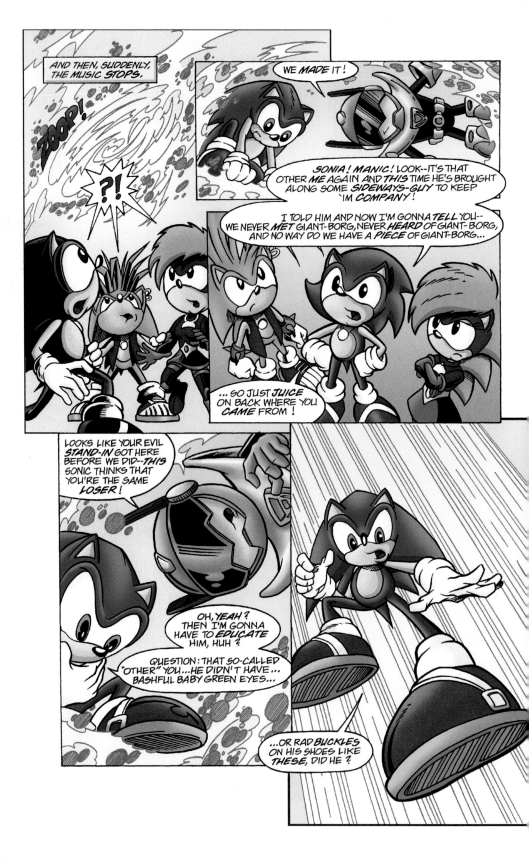

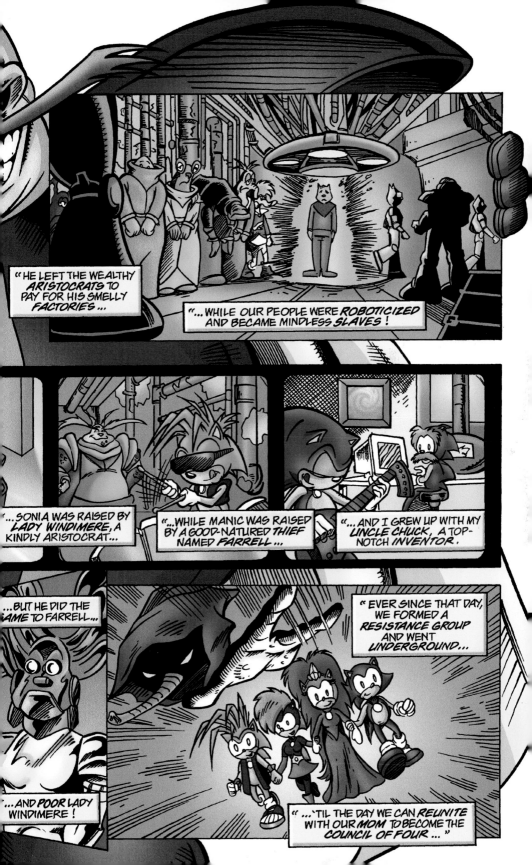

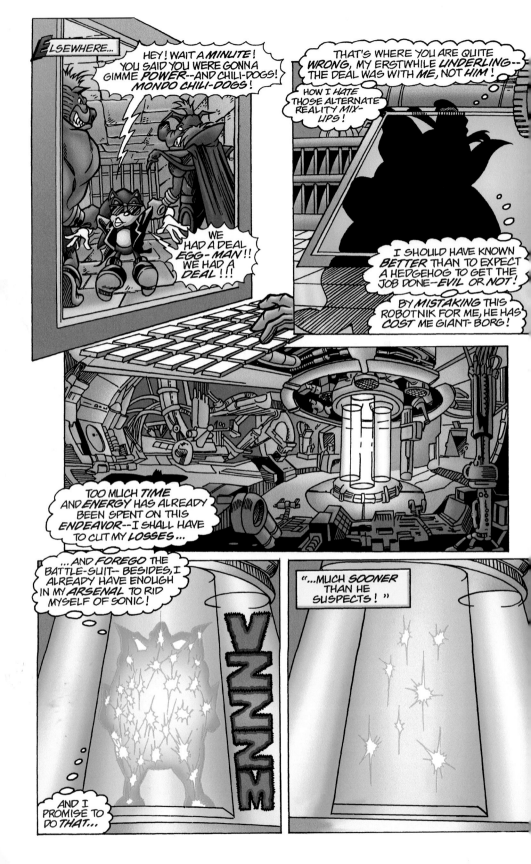

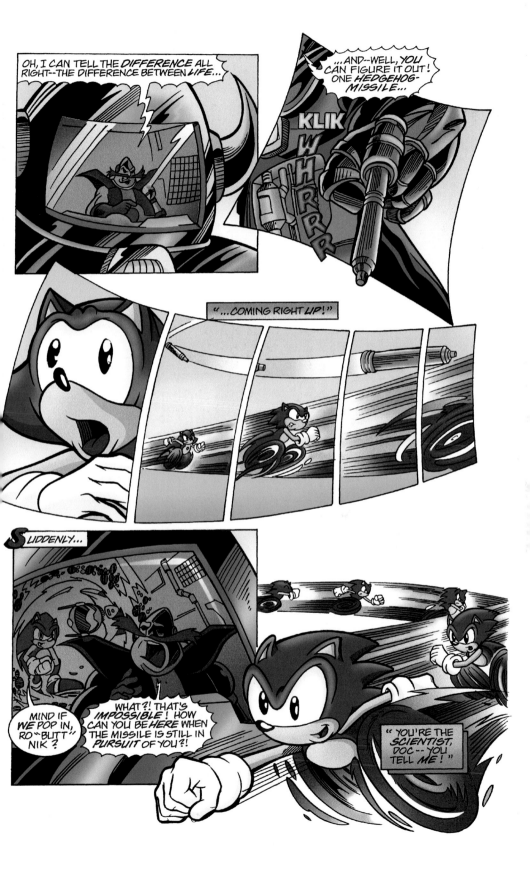

ARE WE GONNA GET FAT *BONUSES*, SLEET?

IT'S NOT EVERY DAY WE CAPTURE SONIC THE HEDGEH--

WHUMP

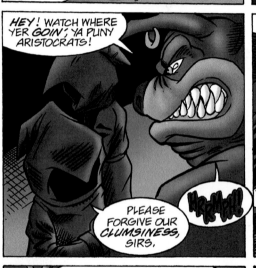

HEY! WATCH WHERE YER *GOIN'*, YA PUNY ARISTOCRATS!

HRRMPH!!

PLEASE FORGIVE OUR *CLUMSINESS*, SIRS.

WHAT THE--?!

WHO THE *HECK* ARE YOU?

HEDGEHOGS WHO'VE COME TO *SAVE* YOU FROM ROBOTNIK'S BRAND OF *JUSTICE*...

IN *FAVOR* OF ANOTHER!

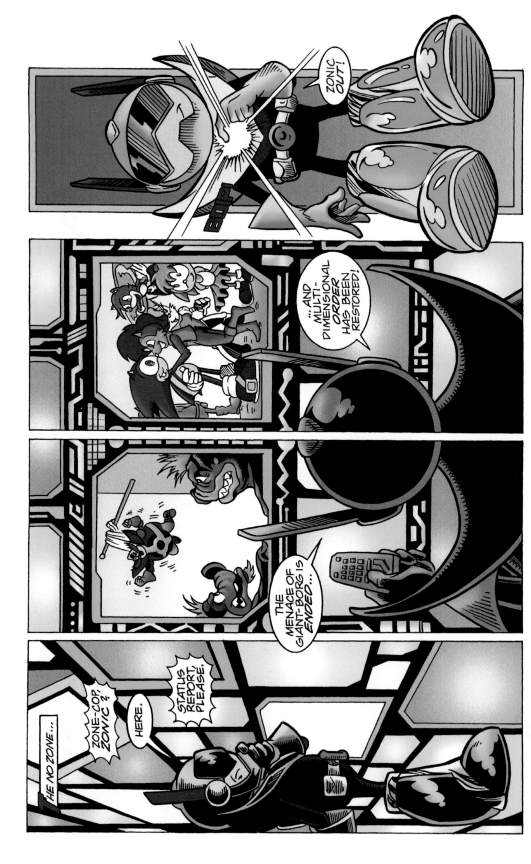

"Zone Wars:
A Tale of Two
Hedgehogs"
Written by Karl Bollers
Illustrated by
Jim Valentino
and Harvey
Mercadoocasio

Lettered by
Vickie Williams

Colored & Separated by
Joshua D. and Aimee R.
Ray

Editor/Art Director
J.F. Gabrie

Managing Editor
Victor Gorelick

Editor-In-Chief
Richard Goldwater

ZONE WARS: GIANT ROBOTNO

Chapter 1

A LAZY AFTERNOON IN KNOTHOLE KINGDOM--

--WHERE A FAMILIAR BLUE *FIGURE* TAKES A MUCH-DESERVED REST FROM FREEDOM FIGHTING.

GONE FISHIN'!

TOO *BAD* HIS TIME OFF--

--IS ABOUT TO BE *CUT* WAY TOO *SHORT*!

LOOP!

YE-OW!

WHAT THE--?!

HELP ME, *SONIC THE HEDGEHOG*-- I'M A *"ZONE"* VERSION OF YOUR OWN ROYAL PRINCESS-- *SALLY ACORN*--

OH, GREAT...

WAITASEC, SONIC--WHAT'S THE *PROBLEM*?

DON'T MEAN TO "*DIS*" YA...

...BUT THIS WHOLE "ZAPPING" ME TO OTHER *ZONES* AND VICE VERSA *ROUTINE*...

...HAS *REALLY* PLAYED ITSELF *OUT*.

LAST TIME IT WAS THAT BUSINESS WITH *GIANT-BORG*...

...AND BEFORE *THAT*, IT WAS *PRETTY SOLDIER SALLY MOON* (AND BOY, WAS SHE *PRETTY*)!

WHAT I'M *SAYING* IS, IT'S TOUGH *ENOUGH* KEEPING AN EYE ON *ONE* PRINCESS SALLY, FORGET *A MILLION* OF HER...

...OR A MILLION ANYONE *ELSES* OUT THERE!

HOW D'YOU KEEP *TRACK* OF IT ALL-- AND *WHY*?

I'VE GOT NO *CHOICE*--

--IT'S MY SWORN *DUTY*.

DON'T YOU *EVER* FEEL LIKE YOU'RE...

...TOTALLY USING *OTHERS* TO GET WHAT YOU *WANT*?

I HELP MAINTAIN COSMIC ORDER BY FIXING ZONAL *INSTABILITIES* ...

...WHICH MEANS PLACING *FOLKS* WHEREVER THEY CAN DO THE MOST *GOOD*.

YOU'RE CALLED ON *MORE* THAN ANY OTHER BECAUSE YOU'RE *SONIC PRIME*-- NUMERO UNO--THE HEROIC *HUB* OF ALL REALITIES!

WELL, I'M *SICK* OF IT! GO FIND *ANOTHER* HUB, *BUB*!

b-dip
b-dip
b-dip

UH-OH! IT'S ANOTHER ZONAL *EMERGENCY* AND ON A SCALE OF ONE TO *TEN*, IT'S AN *ELEVEN*, MILLIONS'LL *PERISH* WITHOUT IMMEDIATE *AID*...

...BUT IF YOU DON'T WANT TO *GO*, I GUESS I'LL HAVE TO *FIND* SOMEONE ELSE *REALLY* QUICK.

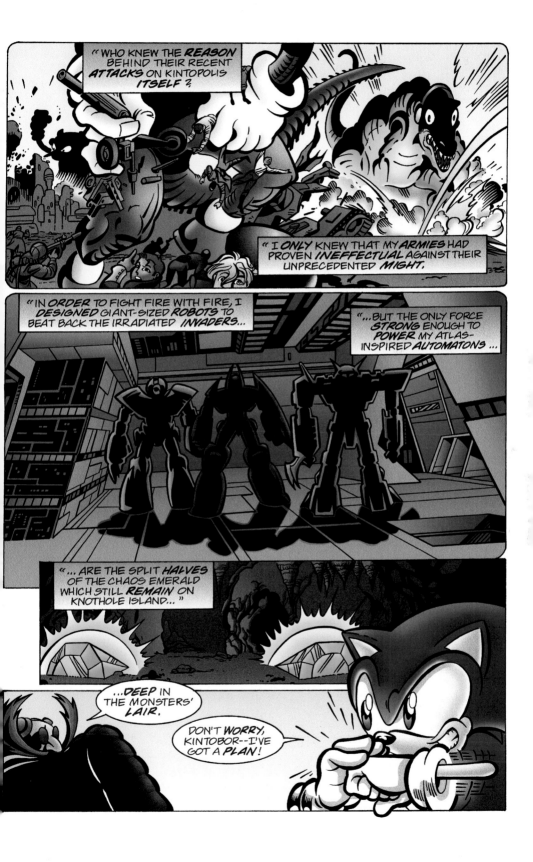

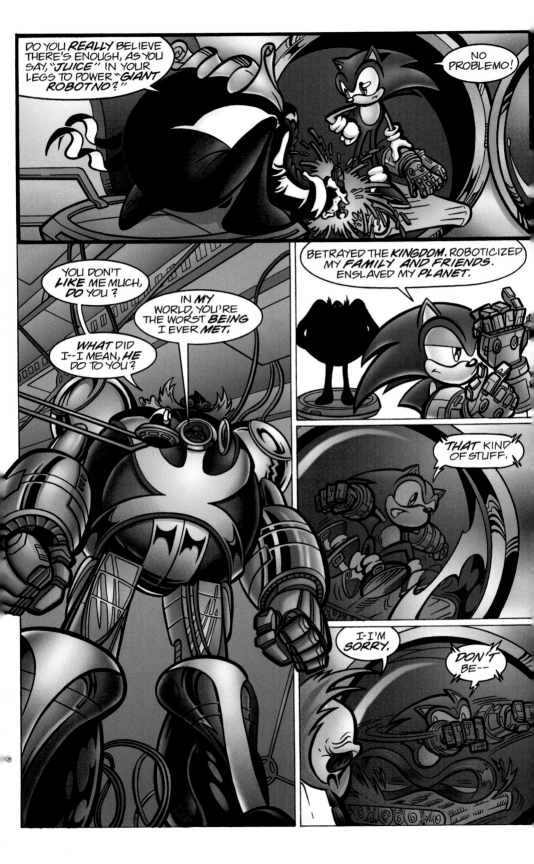

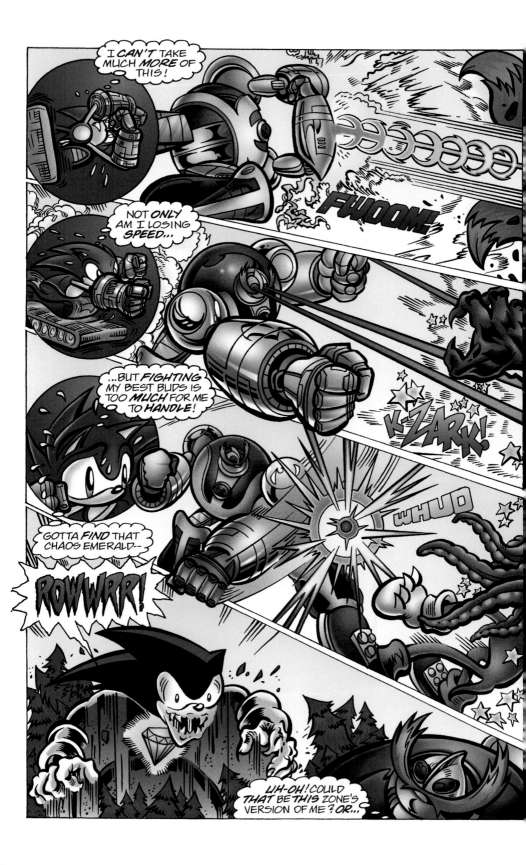

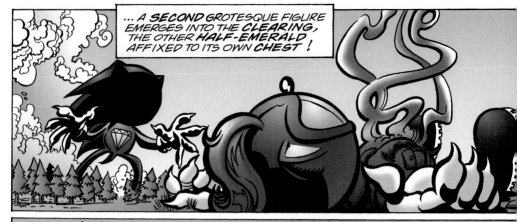

... *A* **SECOND** *GROTESQUE FIGURE EMERGES INTO THE* **CLEARING,** *THE OTHER* **HALF-EMERALD** *AFFIXED TO ITS OWN* **CHEST** *!*

RAARRGH ?

RAAARGGHH!

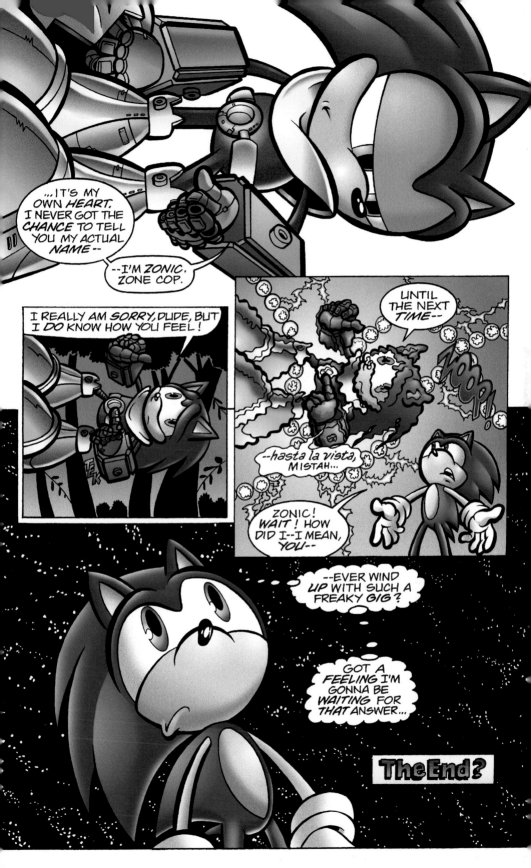

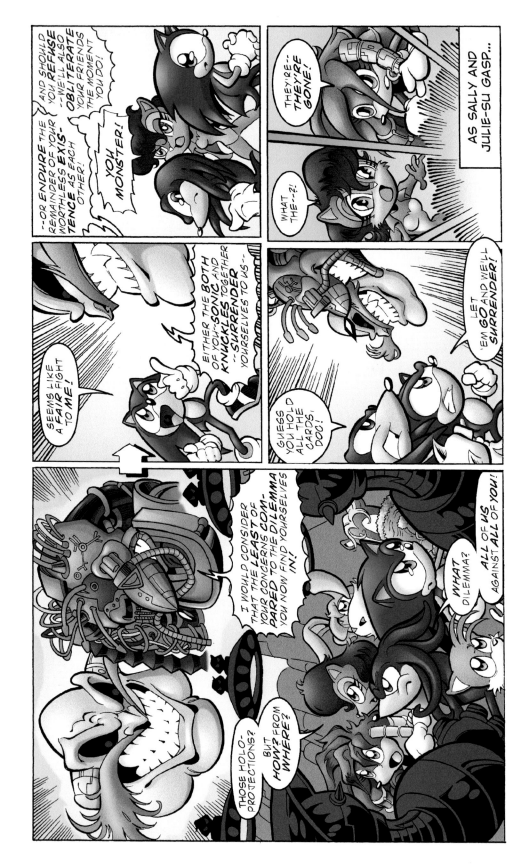

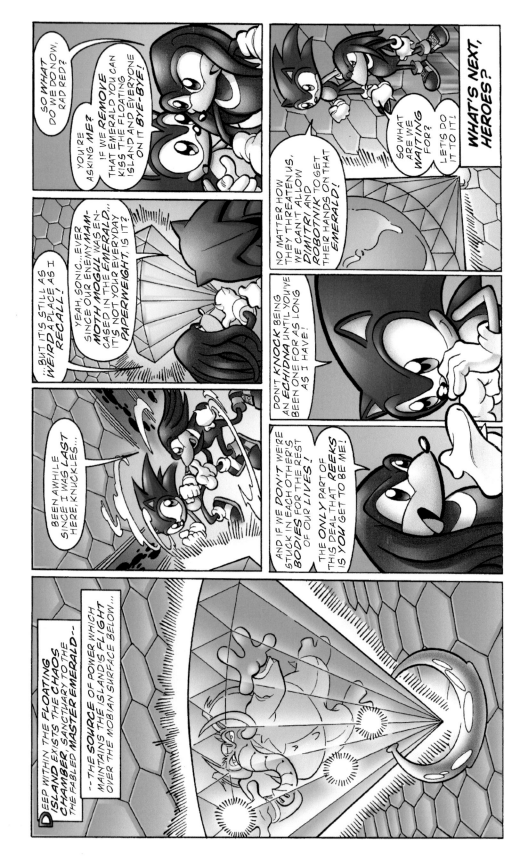

THEIR NUMBERS ARE GREAT, BUT NOTHING I CAN'T HANDLE!

WHAT ABOUT *YOU*, FANG? NEED ANY HELP?

I CAN HOLD MY OWN... BUT IT MIGHT BE STRATEGIC TO MOVE THIS FIGHT TO *HIGHER GROUND!*

Heheheheh! QUITE *BRAVE* OF YOU CHILDREN TO FOLLOW OUR *BACK TRAIL!* LORD *YAGYU* IS SUITABLY IMPRESSED!

IF IT'S THE YAGYU FORTUNE YOU'RE AFTER, YOU'LL FIND THAT IT'S NOT SO *EASILY* TAKEN...

...AND YOU'RE ABOUT TO LEARN WHY!

HEY!!!

GOINK! WE'VE WALKED RIGHT INTO A *TRAP!!*

"--GOOOOOOOD!"

KRA-KA-BOOOOM!

AIIIIIEEEEE!

HA! I KNEW IF I CAUSED ENOUGH TROUBLE, I'D OVERLOAD THAT COMPUTER TYRANT!

HOLD IT RIGHT THERE, CRIMINAL!

YOU'RE UNDER--

AW, PUT A SOCK IN IT!

--OOOOW!

WOW! THANKS!

WHERE'D YOU LEARN HOW TO DO THAT?

WELL, A GIRL'S GOTTA KNOW HOW TO *DEFEND* HERSELF...

CASE CLOSED

-END-

Sonic The Hedgehog has seen some strange places in his day — alternate universes, surreal zones* para-cosmic realities and much more. But none of these could have prepared him for the weirdest one of all... on **Flickie Island!**

Remote and uncivilized, the tiny atoll's unspoiled environment houses more than just the planet **Mobius'** most endangered aviary species, the **Flickie Bird.** The island also contains the secret gateway to the ultimate zone, **The Flickie Zone!**

Unfortunately for the inhabitants of the planet Mobius, the evil **Doctor Ivo Robotnik** has detected this unusual location. He intends to plunder Flickie Island's natural resources to fuel his own nefarious schemes.

And so the stage is set. **Sonic and The Freedom Fighters** must prevent Robotnik from destroying the last pristine eco-system on Mobius — not to mention stopping Ivo's acquisition of the hidden treasure inside the Flickie Zone! But this time, the Doctor is prepared for his enemies... hoo boy, is he prepared!

So, come fly with **The Blue Blur** (and lots of Flickie Birds) as his most incredible adventure yet goes under way...

We guarantee you'll have a — SONIC BLAST!!!

[*The same zones you enter when you play Sonic on your SEGA game systems. - [Editor]

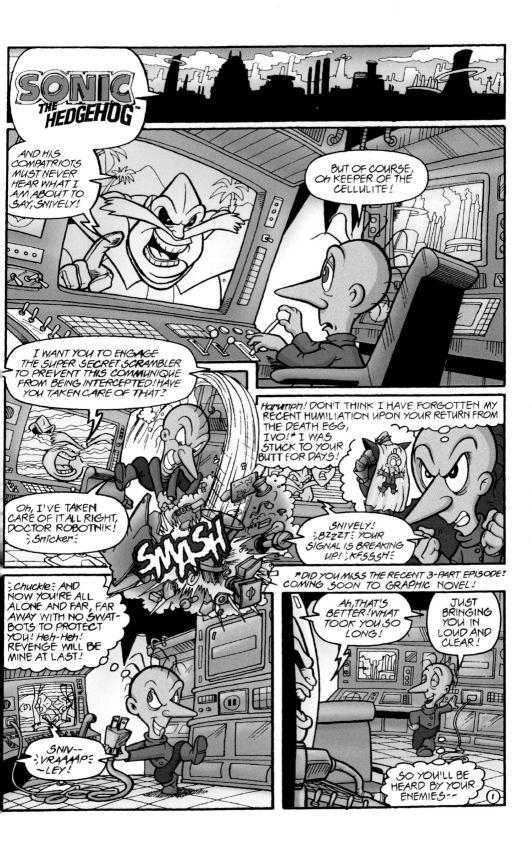

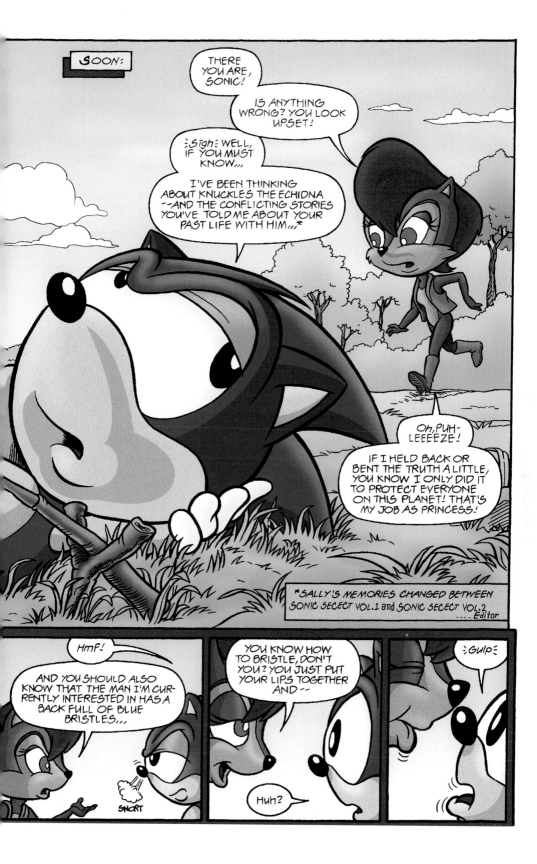

AND SO....

GO FORTH, MY LOVELY FLICKIEBOTS! PATROL THE COASTLINE OF YOUR ISLAND AND KEEP A SHARP EYE OUT FOR INVADERS WHO WOULD *DARE* IMPEDE MY DESTINY!

Flicky!

Flicky!

Flicky!

Flicky!

Flicky!

Flicky!

Flicky!

Flicky!

AND NOW TO FIND A NORMAL FLICKIE BIRD....

....AH, THERE'S ONE NOW!

I'LL SCARE IT AND HE'LL FLY TO SAFETY....

BOO!

Flicky!

ATTABOY! GO FOR THE GREEN!

I'M RIGHT BEHIND YOU! TAKE ME TO YOUR CHAOS EMERALD!

Flicky! Flicky!

7

WRONG AGAIN! THAT WAS THE IMAGE OF ME MOVING AWAY AT DOUBLE LIGHT SPEED! AND NOW FOR A SUPERSONIC WEDGIE!

Yeeeep!

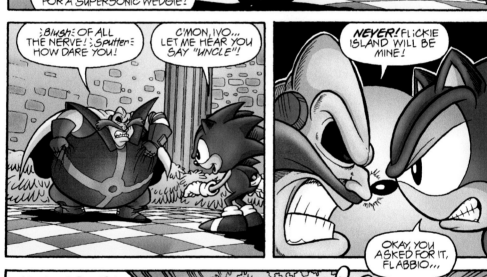

≤Blush≥ OF ALL THE NERVE! ≤Sputter≥ HOW DARE YOU!

C'MON, IVO... LET ME HEAR YOU SAY "UNCLE"!

NEVER! FLICKIE ISLAND WILL BE MINE!

OKAY, YOU ASKED FOR IT, FLABBIO...

NO, YOU DID WHEN YOU ALLOWED OUR NOSES TO MEET! OBSERVE THE NEURAL DISRUPTION FIELD-- TUNED TO MY PHYSIOLOGY, BUT A SHOCKING JOLT TO YOURS!

AGH!

16

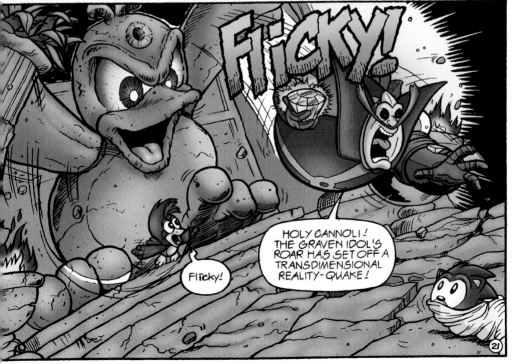

WHOOOHF!

BWONK

COMIN' THROUGH!

HEY! NOT TOO ROUGH! I ALMOST DROPPED THE CHAOS EMERALD!

AAARRR! THE PORTAL RING IS CLOSING! HELP ME, HEDGEHOG!

: Grumble : IT'S HARD TO BE A HERO SOMETIMES...

COME ON ALREADY! STOP WORRYING ABOUT THAT!

OWWWww! Nuh-N-NO! MUST : EEYOWTCH : HAVE EMERALD....

WILL YOU GET OVER IT BEFORE YOU LOSE YOUR ARM?!

BACK INSIDE:

Flicky!

23